GOLFING
SCHOOL

GOLFING
SCHOOL

EDDIE BIRCHENOUGH

PHOTOGRAPHS
BY PHIL SHELDON

BARRON'S

New York • London • Toronto • Sydney

*This book is dedicated to Doug Sanders, the best player
I ever saw*

A QUARTO BOOK

First U.S. edition published in 1989 by
Barron's Educational Series, Inc.
Barron's Educational Series, Inc. has exclusive publication
rights in the English language in the U.S.A., its territories, and
possessions, and Canada.

Reprinted 1989

Library of Congress Cataloging-in-Publication Data
Birchenough, Eddie.
    Golfing school.

    "A Quarto book" — T.p. verso.
    Includes index.
    I. Golf. I. Sheldon, Phil. II. Title
GV965. B549 1989   796.352'3   88-7486
ISBN 0-8120-5793-7

All inquiries should be addressed to:
Barron's Educational Series, Inc.
250 Wireless Boulevard, Hauppauge, New York 11788

This book was designed and produced by
Quarto Publishing plc
The Old Brewery, 6 Blundell Street
London N7 9BH

Project Editors Chris Plumridge, John Andrisani
Senior Editor Kate Kirby

Designer Ted McCausland

Editorial Director Carolyn King
Art Director Moira Clinch

Typeset by Text Typesetters, London
Manufactured in Hong Kong by Regent Publishing
Services Limited
Printed by Leefung Asco Printers Ltd, Hong Kong

CONTENTS

1
PREPARING TO PLAY

2
THE SWING

3
PLAYING WOODS AND IRONS

How to use this book

Where relevant in the teaching sections of this book, graphic devices complement images. These provide an additional commentary on technique. The key is explained below.

The step-by-step sequences are represented by front-on and side-on views to provide an all-round guide to correct posture. For ease of reference, front-on sequences are identified in the captions by upward-pointing triangles △ ; side-on views by side-on triangles ▷.

Direction to exert pressure

Target line

Direction of body turn

Position of head in relation to ball

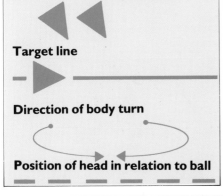

4 MASTERING THE SHORT GAME

5 PUTTING

6 SPECIALIST SHOTS

7

PREPARING TO COMPETE

Goals and Objectives
140•143

Practice
144•149

Competitive Golf
150•155

8

EQUIPMENT

Golf Clubs
158•167

Golf Balls
168•169

Starter Kits
170•171

Clothing
172•173

9

EVOLUTION OF THE GOLF SWING

Goals and Objectives
174•175

From Push to Pull
176•185

FOREWORD

Golf is loaded with people who, like radio announcers, are always sending, never receiving. And going against the trend, Eddie Birchenough found his niche. He became one of the game's great listeners, an essential quality of the great teacher.

We met in 1967, at the British Open at Hoylake, where Eddie was then the assistant club pro. But we did more than meet. I became *aware* of him. He was, quite simply, everywhere. Every time you turned around, Eddie was at the tee, observing, taking notes, waiting to ask a question.

If I practiced at six in the morning or eight at night — my hours were known to be a bit irregular in those days — Eddie was there to watch me swing and to pick my brain. I would explain what I was trying to do, what I had been doing wrong and how I planned to correct it.

Bread upon the waters. Years later, troubled as golfers often are by a mild slump, I could call Eddie and, over the trans-Atlantic phone, listen to him analyze my problem.

Even in the 1960s, he was looking beyond the refinement of his own game. He was interviewing every golfer in sight; even then, I believe, collecting the answers and cataloguing the information that he knew would some day fill a fine and valuable book. And so he has, with the publication of *Golfing School*.

I knew from our first meeting what a serious student of the game he was. He was quiet and patient and professional. Yet he was clearly a man on a mission, searching for anyone who might have a little "magic dust" — anything that might make the swing work better.

Years ago, as a youngster starting out on the PGA tour, I saw Doug Ford hit a sensational choke shot in the Buick Open at Grand Rapids, Michigan. Ford was one of the legendary chippers, and I wanted to learn more about that shot. He had a competitive nature that made it unlikely he would volunteer any trade secrets.

I knew of a small steakhouse where a thick steak cost $3.95 and a carafe of wine was a dollar, and I persuaded the veteran to join a small group of us for dinner. We had a couple of glasses of wine, and I poured him one more for good measure. Then I said, "Doug, I saw you hit that great chip shot today…"

And before I could finish the sentence he said, "Let me tell you what I was thinking." Even in those days, I'd have paid a couple of hundred dollars for that information, but it was mine for about six dollars.

All golfers pick each other's brains. It is a characteristic of the sport. Some of us are less direct than others. With his quiet, attentive approach, Eddie has been equally at ease and equally successful in probing the thoughts of such different personalities as Arnold Palmer, Jack Nicklaus and Lee Trevino.

Our own conversations over the years have tended to focus on the art of shotmaking, which is the essence of golf. On our side of the ocean, we envy the Scottish and British traditions, their infinite variety, the bounce and the run and the lob shots.

I endorse Eddie's theories, and his no-nonsense philosophy, which will benefit golfers of a wide range of skill and attitude. Nor do they exclude those of us who have enjoyed a lifestyle, shall we say, that was less than spartan. In my prime, I would dedicate myself and slave away for half a year. But if, by the time the Tournament of Champions rolled around, I had won enough money to carry me, my reaction was, let the good

times roll.

Yet Eddie and I were, still are, on the same wavelength. There is a special moment – I suppose it applies to any profession – when two people find a harmony of thought. I have seen that spark in Eddie's eye, the way his face lights up, when he asked a question and received the answer he had sought. It is that rare event, the shared moment of communication.

Few of us know instinctively the right questions to ask. Some people can grill you all day and never learn a thing. Someone like Eddie Birchenough can ask one or two of the right ones and an entire history unfolds.

This is his lasting contribution to the game of golf: his 20-year quest to find the information, of getting it out of the heads of the game's distinguished players, and compile it in the pages of a unique book.

Doug Sanders

INTRODUCTION

The origins of golf are shrouded in mystery. There are many forerunners to the game among which are the rustic pastime of the Romans, called *paganica*; the Belgian game *chole* or the sport of *kolfspel* from Holland. All of these games differed in some way from golf, but they all featured that overpowering desire to swing a stick and hit something with it.

Swinging a stick and hitting something with it is now almost a religion for millions of golfers throughout the world. The game provides an irresistible challenge in that it presents the player with innumerable problems during the course of a round, all of which have to be overcome with varying degrees of skill.

Maximizing that skill is the purpose of this book. It is the summation of over 20 years of knowledge in the study and application of the golf swing. Moreover, the technique expounded within these pages reflects the modern approach used by many of the world's most successful professionals. Modern technology has enabled them to analyze every aspect of the swing and to refine it so that it is presented in its simplest form. Obviously, the average player cannot aspire to the same heights as a top professional but the methods of the Golfing School are valid for players of all standards since the basic swing principles do not change.

Finally, I hope that this book will add to your enjoyment of the game by helping you become a better player. Welcome to the Golfing School.

Eddie Birchenough

Eddie Birchenough

PREPARING TO PLAY

A sound golf technique is built on solid foundations. The positions adopted before the swing is triggered dictate the terms of the swing. Therefore, it is vital that the static positions are correct from the outset. These positions include the grip and the way in which the ball is addressed – that is, the stance, the position of the clubhead in relation to the ball and the posture of the body. The importance of assuming these positions correctly cannot be overstressed, because it is from these that good golf stems.

▶ TARGET ◀

To build a sound foundation for the swing by ensuring the fundamentals of grip, stance, posture and balance are correct so that the movement has strength and flexibility.

ACHIEVEMENT

Mental and physical confidence when gripping the club and addressing the ball. An understanding that how the club is gripped dictates the shape of the swing and therefore the type of shot hit.

Tom Watson

Jack Nicklaus and his son Jackie, who often caddies for his father, survey a shot. Many factors have to be taken into consideration before the ball is hit: the distance is calculated from a yardage chart, the direction of the wind is assessed, the position of the pin is verified, the lie of the ball examined and the type of shot needed for the situation is weighed up. Only when all these factors have been clarified will a top professional like Nicklaus select a club and hit the shot.

THE GRIP

Of all the physical actions that take place during a golf swing, gripping the club is by far the most important because you have to control the face of the club if you are to become a competent player. Your grip is your only point of contact with the club, and your ability to control the clubface therefore depends on your ability to grip the club properly. A good grip has to be strong enough to retain control of the golf club throughout the shock of impact, yet it must not be so tight as to restrict the flexibility of the wrists during the swing.

The importance of building a good grip cannot be stressed too strongly. It is critical to good play. Your only contact with the ball is with the clubhead, and the only contact you have with the clubhead is through your hands. The power that is created through the swing is transmitted to the ball through your hands.

Another function of the grip is to balance the relative strengths of your two hands. The typical right-handed golfer who plays at club-level has a much stronger right hand and the function of the grip is to place your left hand in such a position that it is strong enough to dominate the swing.

LEFT-HAND POSITION

Place a club on the ground with the bottom edge of its face pointing toward the target and the shaft of the club tilting slightly toward the target. Hold the club at the top of the handle in the fingers of the left hand. The handle should not lie directly along the roots of the fingers but from the first knuckle of the forefinger to the root of the little finger. Lock the handle in your fingers by applying downward pressure with the pad of the heel of the left hand. This grip applies pressure around the 360 degrees of the shaft, with the possible exception of a few degrees on a line above the fingers and below the palm. Place the thumb along this line so that the grip is totally locked in the left hand. Because the club is tilted slightly toward the target, the heel of the left hand should lie directly on top of the club and the left thumb should be rather more behind the club. This is the strong position referred to earlier, the position that allows the clubhead to be applied with maximum force.

RIGHT-HAND POSITION

It is also the position that allows the left hand totally to dominate the golf swing. With the left hand so strong, the right hand can play only a supporting role, and it should be added to the left as follows: place the right hand immediately below the left on the clubshaft and hold the club in the fingers. You can immediately reduce the power of your dominant right hand by taking your little finger off the shaft, sliding the third finger of your right hand up against the forefinger of your left and laying the little finger across your left forefinger into the crook behind the first knuckle. You are left with the middle two fingers and forefinger holding the shaft, and the middle two fingers of the right hand have the main grip.

⚠ *With the clubshaft tilted slightly toward the target, the left hand has to be placed on top of the club so that it forms a straight line with the left arm. The right hand has to be placed on the grip at the same angle so that the hands complement each other. When the grip is completed, the right thumb will exert a slight downward pressure.*

If you hold the club in your fingers you will find that you can wrap the heel of your right thumb over the top of your left thumb, and, by applying a slight downward pressure, you can make your hands feel as though they are one unit. The right thumb is squeezed against the right forefinger knuckle and forms a bridge over the top of the grip. This bridge is important as it supports the top of the club and helps to lock the clubshaft in the middle two fingers of the right hand. The angle of the palm of the right hand will be parallel to the angle set up by the palm of the left hand, and if both hands were opened and the fingers pointed straight up, both hands would be parallel. Gripping the shaft with

⚠ Because the left hand has been drawn over the top of the club, the club is gripped in the fingers. The fingers are wrapped around the grip, which is held in place by folding the heel of the hand over the top of it. This allows the player to apply pressure around the 360 degrees of the grip, with only a slight weakness along a line at the top of the fingers and the heel of the hand. This is where the thumb should be placed. With the club lying across the fingers, there will, when viewed from behind, be a slight angle between the player's left arm and the club shaft. The angle should be as flat as possible, with the wrist pulled into an arched position.

With the hand placed across the grip in this manner, the left thumb will not reach much further down the shaft than the forefinger. This is known as the short thumb position, and it is a product of the palm and finger grip described here.

⚠ When viewed from the front, the back of the hand, showing three knuckles, will be visible but to the player, whose head is behind the hands, only one and a half or two knuckles will be visible.

When the club is gripped in this manner, the left hand is placed in a dominant position from which it can control the whole swing. The left hand is positioned so that it can transmit maximum clubhead speed into the ball and yet at the same time provide the strength to withstand the tremendous shock of impact.

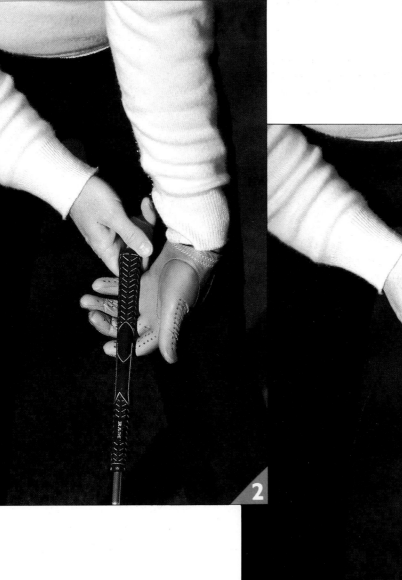

2

3

⚠ To complete the grip the right hand must be added in such a way that it plays a supporting role to the left. This is accomplished by gripping mainly with the middle two fingers of the right hand. The club has to be gripped with these two fingers because they activate the pulling muscles on the inside of the right arm, thereby increasing the overall pulling action of the swing.

4

5

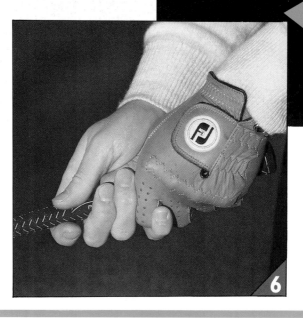

6

⚠ The little finger of the right hand hooks behind the forefinger of the left.

the two middle fingers of the right hand activates a muscle on the inside of the right forearm, and this helps to support the left hand as it pulls the club through the ball at impact.

THE COMPLETED GRIP

When you look down at the completed grip you should be able to see two-and-a-half or three knuckles on the back of your left hand, and the angle of the "V" formed by the right thumb and forefinger. Both will point toward the right shoulder or upper arm.

⑤ Place the roots of the middle two fingers under the grip so that the third finger is next to the forefinger of the left hand. Wrap the fingers around the shaft and fold the right thumb over the left. When viewed from the front, the left thumb will not be visible.

SANDY LYLE

Like all professionals, Sandy Lyle recognizes the fact that the player himself cannot see exactly what he is doing so he needs someone else to reflect the positions he is getting into. All top players have coaches who have an intimate knowledge of their game.

⑦ When the grip is complete, both hands are joined together as a single unit. The hands should be placed as closely together as possible, apart from the right forefinger, which should be triggered down the shaft.

The right thumb is pressed against the lower part of the forefinger forming a bridge over the top of the grip. The forefinger should be wrapped around the grip very lightly because it is not required to add power to the shot.

The top players recognize the importance of having their grips checked, and here Sandy Lyle is being supervised by his father and coach, Alex Lyle.

ADDRESSING THE BALL

The correct address position is one that both provides balance while swinging and aligns the body so that the club can be swung toward the target. The line of the shoulders governs the direction of the arm swing. Therefore the shoulders must be parallel to the target line for the arms to swing down it. The simplest alignment sees the shoulders, hips and feet all parallel to the target line. If the line of the hips and feet point to the left of the target, the stance is referred to as "open." Conversely, if the hips and feet point to the right of the target the stance is referred to as "closed."

If the player assumes an open stance, he will be aware of the target's position because it is still in front of him, and he can adjust his swing accordingly. With a closed stance, the player is placing the target slightly behind himself: this is about as useful as a dart player playing with his back to the board. If a player adopts a square stance, he will naturally be able to swing his arms freely down the target line.

CHOOSING A SITER

If you are to address the ball and aim the club consistently you should develop a routine that will enable you to perform these actions in the same way all the time. Once you have assumed your grip, you should next stand behind the ball and look toward the target. From this position it should be easy for you to visualize the line and the shape of the shot that you want to play. Next, pick out a small mark that is just in front of the ball and on the target line and that you will be able to see when you look down to address the ball. This mark is called a siter. Walk to the ball and, placing the club behind it, aim the blade at the siter. If you are playing an iron shot, aim the bottom of the blade toward the siter – that is, align the blade so that it is at right angles to the line along which you are trying to hit the ball. If you are using a wood, aim the face of the club toward the siter.

When you place the club behind the ball you must lean forward a little, bending from the waist, so that your arms hang clear of your body. Although you should not reach for the ball, make sure you are far enough away from it that your wrists are pulled into a slightly arched position. Because your arms are the same length and your right hand is below the left on the grip, your right shoulder will be slightly lower than the left, tilting the upper body slightly to the right. The right elbow should be tucked in and pointing to the right hip.

22

Left *When you address the ball, as well as considering stance and posture you must also consider other factors such as wind direction and the state of the ground. Your objective is to head straight for the green not for the rough.*

▷*The first act when playing a shot is to aim yourself in the direction you want the ball to fly. The easiest way to do this is to stand directly behind the ball looking toward the target and visualizing the shot you want to play.*

▷ The next step is to place the club behind the ball with the face pointing in the direction in which you want the ball to fly. With the club in this position, bring the right foot forward and measure yourself off the correct distance from the ball.

▷ The left foot is then placed close to the right foot. The required width of stance is achieved by moving the right foot away from the left.

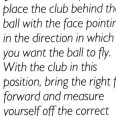

Right When aiming an iron club it is important to place the bottom edge of the clubface at right angles to the target line. This is particularly important with the short irons as these clubs are designed for accuracy.

Above Wooden clubs are easier to aim because the bottom and top edges are virtually parallel. Because woods have a broad, flat sole, they sit naturally on the ground with the face pointing in the right direction.

POSITION OF FEET

Position your right foot first. Point it at right angles to the target line and keep it in this position so that it acts as a governor on the amount of hip turn you can make in the backswing. Then bring your left foot into place, but point it out toward the target slightly to help the hips turn to the left as you swing through the ball.

The weight of your body must be just behind the balls of the feet, just as if you were going to jump straight up into the air. It must never, ever be on the heels, as this tends to lock the ankle, knee and hip joints. If you are in the correct address position, you should be able to feel a slight tension in the calves and thigh muscles. This shows that you are supporting yourself with these muscles and are ready to take part in an athletic movement. With the weight just behind the balls of your feet, you will feel that you will be able to maintain balance while further bending your upper body over. This stance also helps to prevent the chest from obstructing the arm swing.

Hold your head so that your neck is in a straight line with your spine. Your head should be behind the ball, so that you can focus easily on the back of the ball, the part that you are trying to hit.

WIDTH OF STANCE

If you are using a driver, your feet should be about 6 inches further apart than the width of your shoulders. If you are using a 7 iron your feet should be shoulder-width apart and, if you are using a wedge, half shoulder-width apart. The ball should be 4-6 inches inside the left heel with all the clubs except the driver; if you are using a driver, it should be just inside the left heel. Having the ball in this position creates a strong left side, and this is vital if you are going to pull the club through the ball, which is the best method of hitting it. If the ball is placed further forward in the stance, the shoulders are drawn across the line from the ball to the target so that a line through them would point to the left of the target. If the ball is placed too far back, the opposite effect occurs: the shoulders are drawn to the right and aim off to the right when you swing the club. In either case, the arms swing across the target line and cause hook or slice spin on the ball.

There should always be an angle between the clubshaft and the arms. This is because the club is gripped *across* the palms of the hands from the thumb to little finger rather than *down* the palms of the hands from wrists to finger tip. It is impossible to hold the club correctly if you run the grip directly down the line of the arms. If you grip the club at the correct angle, both forearms will be the same distance from the body. If you grip the club with the Vs pointing up toward your left shoulder, your right arm will be higher than your left. If the Vs point down too much toward your right hip, your left arm will be too high. A good grip, therefore, is the basis of the alignment of the swing.

NICK FALDO

Like most top professionals Nick Faldo finds aiming the shot the most consistently difficult thing to do properly. So when practicing he gives himself a visual aid to the correct alignment. Apart from helping Faldo to aim the shot, the club on the ground shows him if his takeaway is starting in the proper direction and, if it is not, whether the club is going too far inside or outside the target line.

Nick Faldo assumes a square stance. Note the club lying on the ground to aid alignment during practice.

THE SWING

2

The chief function of the golf swing is to deliver the clubhead into the back of the ball with the clubface square to the target line and traveling at the maximum speed. Achieving this objective consistently requires that certain simple movements are made during the backswing; these movements in turn create similar responsive movements in the downswing. This chapter discusses these movements so that they can be assimilated easily and put into practice on the course. The final section of this chapter makes it clear that the basic swing principles apply equally to both sexes.

▶ TARGET ◀

To introduce the swing movement. To show how the angles created at address dictate the swing movement and how these angles are unique to each player.

ACHIEVEMENT

By introducing movement, tempo and rhythm into technique the concept of a fluid, continuous swing is created.

Bernhard Langer demonstrates how the pull of his arms through the ball brings the club back inside the target line after the ball has gone. Notice how his hips have remained level with the ground.

Ian Woosnam at the top of his swing and on his way to victory in the 1987 Scottish Open. Notice how the shoulders have fully turned while the hips and legs are resisting the shoulder turn to create maximum coil. It is only by this coiling process that power can be created.

THE BASIC SWING

Golf is played from a stationary position. Apart from croquet, there is no other game played outdoors with a club and a ball, in which the feet are kept in the same position throughout the stroke.

THE TURN

The fact that the feet do not move while the stroke is played has a tremendous limiting effect on the different directions in which you can move. If you are to keep your balance, the only way you can both move and create any real power is by turning. When you think of a turn, you think about turning around an axis. In the golf swing, the axis is not the spine, which is not attached to the ground, but the legs, the only parts of the body that are in contact with the ground. At the point of address, your weight is evenly distributed between both legs. On the turn of your backswing, your weight shifts on to your right leg, and on the turn of your downswing it moves to your left leg.

When you shift your weight and turn like this, you cannot keep your head still. The definition of a "turn" as far as the golf swing is concerned is a twisting movement that keeps your shoulders level with the ground. If either shoulder drops at all, the movement you are making is a tilt and not a turn, and a tilt prevents a proper weight shift.

When you address the ball, both the ball and the club are in front of your body. Therefore, if you turn your body, the club will finish up behind it. When you make your backswing turn and turn your left shoulder over your right

leg, the whole of your body weight will be transferred to your right leg. Then, when you make your downswing and swing the club back to the end of the follow-through, your body weight moves in the same direction as the club, supporting the hit and allowing your weight to flow freely on to your left leg into the follow-through. This is a very important sequence, as it allows the golfer to get all his weight into the stroke and to get the maximum energy into the ball that his swing can produce.

When the body turns, the club also turns, so when the shoulders turn 90 degrees to the right in the backswing the face of the club will also have turned 90 degrees to the right. By the time the club has reached hip height and is parallel to the ground the toe of the club should be pointing vertically up into the air. Do not try to keep the clubface toward the target throughout the swing.

BACKSWING

The first movement of the backswing should be the pushing of the left hand and arm away from the target. It will feel as if the club is moving straight back, but, as the club is being swung in an arc around the shoulders, the clubhead will come a little inside the target line almost immediately. If the backswing is checked when the club shaft is parallel to the ground, the shaft should also be parallel to the target line. This ensures that the plane of the swing is established on the target line. The plane is the angle between the ball and the player's shoulders. No golfer has a choice

To illustrate the role of the shoulders in the swing, hold a club across the upper chest △. Turn the shoulders to the right △2 and back again to the left

△3 without allowing the club to tilt toward the ground. This demonstrates that when the shoulders turn, they rotate level with the ground.

of which plane to swing in, as this is determined by his height, the length of his arms and his distance from the ball. Once these criteria are established, the angle of the plane inevitably follows.

THE POWER SOURCE

The feeling of the first part of the backswing is of pushing the club straight back from the ball with the left hand and arm. By the time the club is horizontal to the ground at hip-height, the shoulders will have been pulled around by the swing of the left arm, but the hips will still be in their original address position and will not move until the turn of the shoulders pulls them around. This coiling of the muscles between the hips and the shoulders is a major power source, which is eliminated if the hips are turned too early. As the left arm continues to swing back, the shoulders are pulled around in front of the face. The left shoulder is pulled across to the right and should not tilt: this movement of the shoulders creates the weight shift on to the right side of the body. If you tilt your shoulders the weight drops vertically on to the left hip and leg and causes the reverse pivot.

At the end of the backswing the golfer should feel further from the ball because the left shoulder has not

By the time the clubhead has reached shoulder height in the backswing △, the shoulders will have been pulled around nearly 90 degrees, but the hips will have been left behind in the position they were at address △. This movement stretches the muscles in the left side between shoulder and hip.

31

dropped. The hands should still be in the same positon in relation to the arms as they were at address: if the left hand and arm were in a straight line at address, they will remain so. There should be no change throughout the swing.

DOWNSWING

With the left hand and arm in line, the left hand lies above the right ready to dominate the downswing with a pull. Keeping the hands in this position ensures that the face of the club works within the plane of the swing that was established at address and all that is required of the downswing is that the clubface is pulled through the ball; no squaring up is necessary. You cannot pull the club squarely through the ball from a cupped-wrist position at the top of the backswing; you have to use the right hand to square up the clubface.

The backswing has concentrated effort on the top half of the body, and when you reach the top of the swing you will be mainly aware that the muscles on the left side between the shoulder and the hips are being stretched. In fact, how far you turn is less important than how far you stretch. A tall, slim person will use less hip turn than a shorter, stockier person. When the club is pushed back by the left hand and arm, the right elbow folds nicely into the side. Because the right elbow was pointing to the right hip at address, the right wrist is allowed to cock properly at the top of the backswing. The wider stance that was assumed at address helps to limit the amount of hip turn in the backswing, which means that at the top of the swing, the top half of the body is turning on a firmer platform.

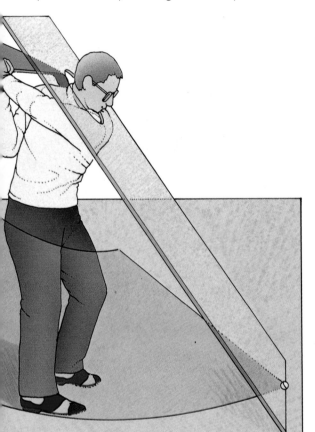

Left *The most graphic illustration of the plane of the swing. By imagining a pane of glass and the swinging of the club underneath it, the player is able to establish the correct angle at which to swing the club.*

Above *It is easy to see that it is necessary to swing the club at a shallow angle to prevent shattering the glass. The fact that the bottom of the pane of glass points to the target establishes the path the clubhead should follow.*

THE SWING PLANE

The plane of the swing is the angle of the arc on which the club is swung. As we have seen, the club is swung straight back from the ball, but, because the golfer stands to the side of the ball, the club is swinging around his body. The perfect illustration of this part of the golf swing was made by Anthony Ravielli in Ben Hogan's book *Modern Fundamentals of Golf*. Ravielli drew a pane of glass with a hole in it; the golfer's head came through the hole with the glass resting on his shoulders. The lower edge of the pane lay on the line along which the ball was going to be hit. When the club was swung, it swung underneath the pane of glass all the way through the backswing and all the way through the downswing as well. I believe that notwithstanding Hogan's many victories and the heights to which he ascended to become such a magnificent striker, possibly his greatest contribution to golf was his analysis of the swing plane.

PULLING THROUGH THE BALL

The length of backswing is relatively unimportant. What is important is to turn the shoulders as far as possible while stretching the muscles on the left side. The shoulders usually turn about 90 degrees, and, if the muscles at the left side are fully stretched, the hips will turn between 30 and 45 degrees, nowhere near as much as the shoulders. When the hips are turned in this way, they pull the left leg across and toward the right leg, and the left heel comes slightly off the ground as the whole body weight is transferred to the right side. A supple person does not need to lift his left heel from the ground at all, but a stockier person may find that his heel needs to come up as much as 2 inches.

As the shoulders are pulled around at the start of the backswing, the club swings behind the body. The sooner the shoulders turn in the backswing, the sooner the club comes away from the target line and swings behind the player. If a player swings the club straight back from the ball directly along the target line, the line on which his arms are pulled in the backswing does not require him to turn his shoulders, and he will lift the club with just his arms and hands. This will lead to a very steep downswing, and the club will approach the ball from almost directly above it. Such a movement is a classic recipe for a slice or a topped shot. The shoulders should turn first in the backswing and drag the hips around only when the maximum stretch has been achieved by the muscles on the left side.

There is, in fact, no such thing as a "position" at the top of the backswing. Instead the shoulders coil up and stretch the left side as far as they can, and then the downswing is started when the hips turn to the left and increase the stretch of the left side, eventually dragging the shoulders, then arms and finally the clubhead through the ball. The hips will return before the shoulders because they did not turn as far in the backswing. This initial pull moves the weight on to the left leg, and the hips continue to move the shoulders, arms and hands through the ball toward the target. The power source is now in the hips; so the club will try to find the plane around the hips that makes the club move downward and sets up a shallower attack on the ball.

THE FULL SWING

uring the downswing the dominant force is centrifugal. This means that the energy in the club travels along the shaft line. Force does not travel at right angles to the shaft; so it is not possible for the right hand to add power: it can only adjust the alignment of the face. Your head, meanwhile, must stay behind the ball until after impact; you will not be able to keep it totally still, of course, but it must be behind the ball. Many of the very best players move their heads away from the target in the downswing because their bodies are setting up a force that opposes the pull of the arms.

POSITION OF FEET AND HIPS

As we have already seen, the feet remain in the same place throughout the golf swing; therefore power is created by turning. The sensation during the downswing is of pulling the hips to the left, and you should try to keep your hips as far ahead of the shoulders as they were at the top of the backswing. At that point the ball is in front of you and the clubhead behind you; so if all you do is pull with the left side the club must approach the ball from inside the target line.

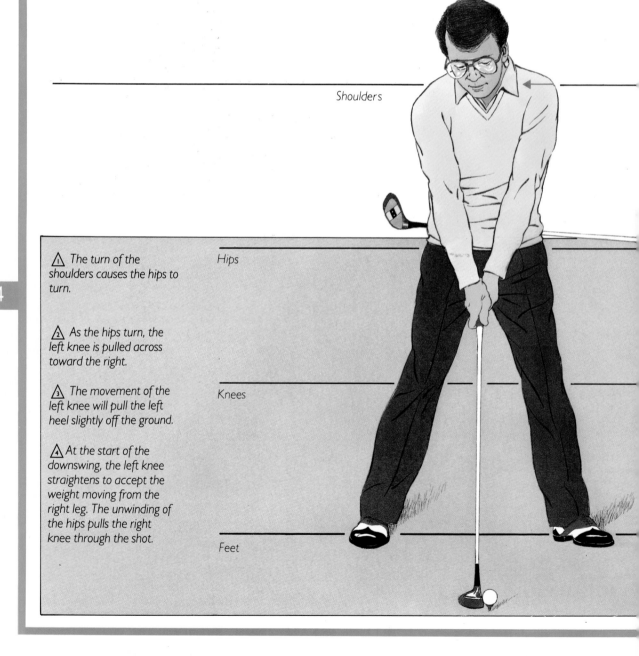

Shoulders

Hips

Knees

Feet

△1 The turn of the shoulders causes the hips to turn.

△2 As the hips turn, the left knee is pulled across toward the right.

△3 The movement of the left knee will pull the left heel slightly off the ground.

△4 At the start of the downswing, the left knee straightens to accept the weight moving from the right leg. The unwinding of the hips pulls the right knee through the shot.

34

THE IMPORTANCE OF A SHALLOW ATTACK

After impact, the hips keep pulling the club toward the target in a wide arc, and this delays the crossing over of the hands. The right hand will pass the left at about shoulder height on the follow-through as the arms swing around the shoulders, which should be level at the end of the swing. The left side will be straight. The hands will be in the same relationship to the left shoulder at the end of the follow-through as they were to the right shoulder at the top of the backswing. During the through swing, attention focuses on the lower half of the body, the legs and the hips.

The shallow attack on the back of the ball is important because you are trying to hit the ball forward, and to hit the ball forward you must hit it on the back. A shallow attack allows you to do this. If you were to make a steep attack, the hit on the ball would be downward and power would be lost.

In the course of the downswing the dominant force is centrifugal. This is the force that uncocks the wrists and widens the angle between the clubshaft and the left arm during the downswing. This uncocking action brings the club into a straight line, with the left arm directly below the left shoulder, and beyond that point the clubhead swings past the hands.

When this happens and the arc begins to diminish, the clubhead is pulled in against that force and slows down very quickly. The clubhead accelerates only until the point that the left arm and the clubshaft become a straight line;

1

2

there, the ball must be struck before this position is assumed. That is why, at address, it is an excellent idea to rehearse this position by gripping the club with the shaft tilted slightly forward and with the hands in front of the clubface and above the ball.

It is the first rule of golf that at the moment of impact the hands must be in front of the ball; they must be nearer to the target than the ball. Doing this guarantees that the club is accelerating into the ball at the moment of impact and therefore produces the most powerful blow that you can present to the ball. As we saw earlier, this can be achieved consistently only by pulling the club on to the ball.

THE RELEASE

Halfway through the downswing a player in the classic position will have fully cocked wrists and the toe of his club will be pointing up into the air. He is unwinding his body and turning it to the left so that the club will also turn to the left. Thus, at the corresponding position at shoulder height in the follow-through, the club will have turned through 180 degrees and the toe of the club will be pointing up in the air again. This is the action that many top players call "the release," as it releases the clubface through the ball. This is a very important aspect of the golf swing, and, by learning to do it consistently, a player not only learns to hit the ball far

Shoulders

Hips

Knees

Feet   3   4 and straight but also learns where the clubface is pointing through the critical area of the swing so that by making only slight adjustments he can make the ball slice to the right or hook to the left at will.

The head should stay behind the ball after the impact only until the turn of the shoulders pushes it up and the body straightens to become erect at the end of the follow-through. It is also necessary to lift the head at this point so that the flight of the ball can be watched.

When the shoulders turn away from the ball at the beginning of the backswing, a golfer may feel that he is turning on an absolutely level plane. This is not so,

however, because the spine is tilted forward at address and the shoulders turn at right angles to the spine. Nevertheless the idea of turning in a level plane helps to keep the left shoulder up and keeping the left shoulder high and turning it causes the clubface to open naturally in the backswing, and allows the player to keep the club within the plane of the swing. The left shoulder stays up as it turns into the backswing, and it follows that during the down-swing the right shoulder will not be pulled down but will instead be pulled around the head in the same plane that the left shoulder took in the backswing. This position will make the player more aware of his arms swinging down

5

6

and through the ball into the follow-through.

When the body weight is established on the left side and the hips have turned to the left in the downswing, the right leg is also pulled through the shot. This action causes the right heel to lift off the ground just before impact, and no attempt should be made to keep it clamped on the ground. At the end of the classic swing, the right foot should not be carrying any weight, and the heel should be vertically above the toes.

The power in the swing is created by stretching the muscles down the left side. The more the hips are left behind in the address position while the shoulders make their maximum 90 degree turn, the tighter the muscles are drawn and the more recoil there will be in the downswing. The purpose of the downswing is to turn the left hip and maintain the stretch in the left side so that at impact the left side is stretched just as much as it was at the top of the backswing.

ROLE OF THE HANDS AND WRISTS

The role of the hands, or rather, the action of the wrists, throughout the golf swing is of great importance. The takeaway is performed with the left hand pushing the club away from the target. As the shoulders turn and the right

Shoulders

Hips

Knees

Feet

7

8

elbow folds into the right side, the wrists cock to accommodate this movement. At the top of the backswing the angle between the left arm and the club shaft is usually about 90 degrees, because the back of the left arm and the back of the left hand are in the same relationship to each other as they were at address. When the left hip starts the downswing towing of the left shoulder and arm, the weight of the clubhead forces the wrists to cock even more. This extra cock at the start of the downswing helps to create a late hit. It totally eliminates the early throw of the club with the right hand, which is the bane of many a handicapped golfer. The greater the wrist cock at this point in the downswing, the later the release will be into the ball, and the further the ball can be hit. This is the explanation for why many slightly built or short players can out-hit even the tallest golfers: they are unable to uncock their wrists late in the downswing.

This uncocking is not a conscious movement. The pull of the left arm and the centrifugal force working upon it automatically uncock the wrists. The extra cocking at the start of the downswing merely delays the moment before centrifugal force gets to work. The later the hit through the ball, the later in the follow-through the clubhead passes the hands, and the later the crossover point. This is another factor in great shot-making accuracy. There is no doubt that the greatest players are those who hit the ball with the latest possible release of the wrists through the impact area.

After the hands have crossed over, they swing naturally around the player's shoulder as far as they can go to the end of the swing. At no point of the downswing is there a conscious hit with the right hand.

△5 The shoulders respond to the unwinding of the hips by maintaining a level plane as the club swings through the ball. The hips create the thrust of the downswing by turning to the left and transferring the weight to the left leg.

△6 The body weight is transferred from the right foot to the left during the downswing and, as the body clears, the right foot is pulled on to the toe.

△7 The rotation of the arms after impact allows the shoulders to continue to turn in a level plane.

△8 The hips, which led through the downswing, have turned to the left as far as they can go.

△9 The left leg is straight and the weight is on the left foot.

9

LONG SWINGS AND SHORT SWINGS

The length of the backswing is not important. Far more important is how much you stretch the left side of your body. Swinging the club back until the shaft is horizontal to the ground at the top of the backswing does not make any difference at all. In general, the longer the swing, the higher the ball is hit, and the shorter the swing, the more the ball seems to be propelled forward, which is the way it needs to be propelled if maximum distance is to be attained.

To get the club back into a horizontal position, most golfers either have to let go of the grip, over-turn their hips or lift their left foot off the ground so that it rests only on the very tip of the toes at the top of the backswing. These are all faults. A player with a shorter swing has the club under control at all times and is able to concentrate on swinging the club forward and into a long follow-through rather than having to recover from a faulty backswing position.

Among the longer swingers over the last 15 to 20 years are renowned professionals such as Tom Watson, Johnny Miller and Ben Crenshaw. Nevertheless, while all three of them are brilliant iron players, none could be described as a consistent driver. This is because the long swing that they feel they need to give them distance also makes them erratic. When they use shorter shafts in their irons, the swing becomes controllable and they are brilliant. I do not suppose anybody has hit good iron shots more consistently than Johnny Miller did in the early 1970s. He did not just hit the ball close to the hole, he used to lean it against the flagstick.

However, if you compare the number of fairways hit by Miller, Watson and Crenshaw with those hit by Peter Jacobsen, Doug Sanders and Lee Trevino, probably three of the game's shortest swingers. Jacobsen, Sanders and Trevino will have hit twice as many fairways as the other three players. In fact, they are still able to play more attacking shots to the green because they play from the short grass of the fairways almost all of the time. If the longer swingers all hit the ball 100 percent and the shorter swingers all hit the ball 100 percent, the longer swingers would probably hit the ball further over the course of a round, but the shorter swingers would drive more shots onto the fairway.

THE MODERN SWING

Swing the club away from the ball with your left hand and arm and turn your shoulders as far as you can before allowing your hips to move. When you feel you are losing balance or you have to let go of the club to keep it going further, that is the point at which your backswing should stop. As long as your arms get up to about shoulder height and your shoulders turn as far as they can while stretching your left side away from your hip, that is as long a backswing as you need, because you are still in control of the club. Pull with your left side and keep your left hand in front of the clubhead throughout impact, and you will hit the ball as the club accelerates, and that means that you will be transmitting the maximum power into the ball through the clubhead and achieving the maximum distance you are capable of with that club.

There are only two ways to move an object – you can push it or you can pull it. In golf it is essential that you pull your club through the ball if you want to achieve consistency and power. This is the modern swing. This is the swing that has been evolved by trial and error over the years by the game's greatest players. It is a method that does not let them down in the pressures of tournament play. It is the method that allows them consistently, day in and day out, to compete for the huge amounts of money that are available to the top players these days.

THE WEIGHT SHIFT

It is worth spending more time on the shifting of weight during the swing. As the club is swung back from the ball by the left arm and shoulder at the beginning of the backswing, the movement of the club to the right should take the body weight firmly across on to the right side. By the time the club has been swung to hip height, 80 percent of the body weight is firmly on the right foot.

This move must be established right at the start of the backswing to ensure that the right leg is a firm foundation on which the upper body can turn. As long as the left shoulder turns on a plane level with the ground, the single movement of turning the left shoulder across and over the right leg will transfer the weight to the right leg. As we want the shoulder turn to be complete by the time the hands have swung up to shoulder height, this movement must be completed in the first half of the backswing. At the top of the backswing the weight must be on the right side so that, when the arms are swung forward through the ball on the downswing, the body weight is moving in the same direction as the club, thereby supporting the hit and making the strength of the strike so much more solid. This weight shift also helps to keep the body erect throughout the stroke.

Many golfers resist this weight movement to the right side because when they do make the correct movement,

▷ As the club is swung away from the ball, the clubface will rotate with the turn of the shoulders.

they feel as if they are swaying to the right. Remember, in a golf swing, because your feet are anchored, the only way you can move to make any energy at all in the backswing is with a turn, and if you are turning with your weight on your right leg you cannot possibly sway.

If the left shoulder does not stay high as it turns into the backswing but tilts down toward the ground, the right hip will be forced to move to the right, thereby taking away the height that your body has established at address and moving the center of your arc closer to the ground. This will cause you to hit the ground behind the ball. Because the left shoulder has dropped and the right hip slid to the right at the top of the backswing, the weight has been dropped down through the left hip on to the left foot, and the body

Right and below right
The angle between the back of the left hand and the arm at address must be maintained throughout the swing. This way the clubface maintains a constant relationship with the body.

▷ *Halfway back, the shoulders and the clubface will both have turned 90 degrees.*
This rotation of the blade helps to keep the left shoulder high and in the downswing, will allow the player to release the right side through the shot.

▷ *The turn of the shoulders brings the club inside the target line. This turning action keeps the right arm close to the side of the body, which is a very strong position.*

41

will be bowed out to the right with the weight on the left foot – there will have been no weight shift to the right.

The weight shift to the right causes the downswing to become shallow and enables you to attack the ball with the club traveling in a much wider arc. Again, the weight shift to the right will give a feeling of having more room to swing in. Shifting your weight to the right leg enables your arms to swing more freely.

When the weight shift is properly executed, it requires that the lower half of the body, the legs and the hips are used properly. Players often say that they cannot use their legs in the golf swing, and they never will until they learn to shift their weight properly. As soon as they learn to transfer their weight to the right leg in the backswing and

through onto the left leg in the follow-through, their leg action will fall into place.

WEIGHT SHIFT'S EFFECT ON TEMPO
A good weight shift also gives the golf swing a constant tempo. It is very easy to swing the club too quickly if you are swinging only with your arms and hands, but it is very difficult to shift the mass of your weight quickly as this has to be done by the large muscles in the body. The weight shift acts as a governor on the pace at which you can swing to the top of the backswing because it takes so long for the weight to shift on to the right leg and because the weight shift has to be complete by the time the hands are at shoulder height in the backswing. The time taken to make a

42

▷ Halfway through the downswing in the perfect position the wrists are fully cocked and the toe of the club points straight up in the air.

▷ To use this position properly, the golfer has to rotate the arms as the wrists uncock.

▷ By the time the club has reached shoulder height in the follow-through, it will have turned to the point where the toe is pointing up in the air again.

This rotation of the clubface is known as the release. The full release of the clubface in this manner gives power and direction to the shot. It also ensures that after impact, the club stays in the plane used for the back- and downswings.

▷ At the finish of the swing the club lies over the left shoulder at the same angle it lay over the right shoulder at the top of the backswing.

hand swing up to shoulder height is kept at a constant, slow pace to allow the body time to make the weight shift. When the weight shift is complete, the shoulders and arms coil tighter up to the top of the backswing.

The downswing is initiated when the left hip pulls to the left and the weight is pulled on to the left leg. This is also an action that takes place relatively slowly, and it allows the clubhead, which is still moving back, to tighten the coil even more as the lower body starts down. When the weight is established and balanced on the left leg, it acts as a solid base from which the club can be pulled through the ball in the downswing. This is one reason why the hips must turn in the downswing and not move laterally to the left. If they do move laterally to the left, they tend not to take the

weight with them. Instead, the weight remains on the right leg, which causes the right shoulder to drop behind the ball. When this happens, the hit becomes a scoop. The follow-through is created by the hands and arms becoming disconnected from the body and being lifted over the head. This exaggeratedly high position forces the body into the incorrect reverse-C position. Ensuring that the downswing is made predominantly by the hips turning to the left, the body will stay upright. As the body remains upright the weight is transferred more freely on to the firm left leg.

The importance of the weight shift is being increasingly understood and is being taught by the more discerning of the top teaching professionals. It is an entirely natural

7

6

SEVE BALLESTEROS

Seve Ballesteros is capable of hitting more different kinds of shots to order than any other golfer in the world. His swing control is so good that he is able to alter the alignment of the clubface slightly and produce any type of flight a shot requires.

movement. If you were to throw a stone, you would shift your weight without thinking about it.

WOMEN GOLFERS

Although women are less physically strong than men, there is no reason why they should be at a disadvantage when playing a game like golf. Most women do not play as well as men, not because of a lack of distance but because they do not pay enough attention to their short game. Because they are physically weaker than men, it is important that women use in their golf swing the large muscles in their backs and legs so that they maximize the power they have in their bodies to create distance. It is essential that women are taught to turn their shoulders more than their hips and that their weight shifts and coils on the right side at the top of the backswing. Only by winding those large muscles in the back and legs can women hope to maximize their power and turn it into length.

One problem that women often have as they try to swing is their bosom. When the proper turn is made away from the ball at the start of the backswing, the whole of the upper body turns, and by the time the arms want to swing on their own, the bosom has been turned out of the way and the left arm can swing up and behind the body. Women golfers who find their bosom impedes their ability to swing their arms are definitely not turning their shoulders properly.

Because they tend to lack distance from the tee, many women golfers have become very proficient fairway players. Most would prefer to play with a 3, 5 or even a 7 wood than with a 3, 4, or 5 iron because they don't hit the ball hard enough to compress it sufficiently to get the backspin that makes the ball fly high in the air with a long iron shot. They wisely select the fairway woods, which allow them to sweep the ball high into the air with a minimum of effort.

Where many women golfers fall down is within 50 yards of the green. They often seem to lack judgment of distance, a control over trajectory and the ability to hit the ball the required distance along the ground on the greens. There are few outstanding women putters. It may be that some women do not like to be seen to be competitive and therefore ignore the attractions of the practice putting green. However, because the shots inside 50 yards do not require great physical strength, there is no reason why women, with practice, cannot be just as good at these shots as a man. Indeed, with practice, I would expect a woman player to develop better and more quickly than a man because she is more sensitive to these little shots close to the green.

At the top level, women golfers play with about the same sort of strength as an average man, and many men golfers would benefit immensely by going to a tournament and watching how the great women professionals play.

It is noticeable that the best women players over recent years have started to play with lighter shafts in their clubs. On the women's tour in Europe, graphite clubs are very common, and many professionals have found that these lightweight shafts have increased their distance potential. Many of the women are using perimeter-weighted clubs

At address the female golfer will stand with her hands higher to create more room for her arm swing $\triangleright$.
Apart from that, the same swing principles apply. She will position her hands slightly ahead of the ball, *with her left hand turned over the shaft in the strong position $\triangle$. Her weight will be balanced toward the balls of her feet, enabling her calf and thigh muscles to support her weight.*

because the weight of the sole of the club helps them to elevate their long iron shots. This extra loft helps them to control the ball. Because they lack men's distance, many of the women professionals play with a two-piece ball or with a surlyn-covered ball. Because they are weaker hitters, they require less backspin on their shots than their male counterparts. When they want to loft a shot they have to do it with the loft on the club rather than by spinning the ball. For this reason, many of them are probably using 60 degree loft on their wedges as standard practice.

Women tend to swing the club back further than men, partly because they are more supple than men and partly because they need to try to create greater length. They seem to believe that if they swing back further, they will hit the ball further. This is not true, although the extra length of their swing does tend to make them more graceful; but they are not nearly so powerful when they swing through the ball. Because of their long swing, with its gradual acceleration from the top to impact, women need a softer, more flexible shaft in their clubs as an additional aid to making the ball fly up into the air.

Any woman golfer who wants to improve her game

Because women are more supple than men they find it easier to turn their shoulders in the backswing.

They usually require less hip turn to accomplish this. A full shoulder turn eliminates the need to overcock the wrists. The full shoulder turn transfers the weight to the right leg and places the club in a position to make a shallow attack on the back of the ball ⚠. Their lack of power means that the ball must be driven forward, and only a shallow angle of strike can achieve this.

is essential for women olfers to turn their houlders at the start of the ackswing ▷ ⚠

Top row At impact she has rotated the clubface so that it is square to the target [5]. Halfway into the follow-through the club has continued to rotate so that the toe is again pointing into the air [6].

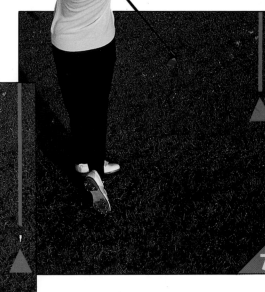

The extra suppleness of women is shown at the end of the swing. The club has traveled in a much longer arc than it would in the case of a male player ▷. This long follow-through helps the woman player to sweep the ball up into the air.

should work hard on getting the proper grip on the club. Then she should concentrate on turning properly away from the ball – on keeping the shoulders level to the ground, on allowing the weight to be transferred on to the right leg at the start of the backswing and on coiling the shoulder sway from the hips so that at the top of the backswing the muscles in the left side between the shoulder and the hip are drawn tight. The turn away from the ball during the swing inhibits many women players. They should not swing the club back from the ball too quickly or they will build up so much momentum in the head of the club that when they get to the top of the backswing the club will simply pull itself out of their hands. The tempo of the swing must be gentle; it should be taken at the same rate as the weight shift going back on to the right leg to ensure that the club arrives at the top smoothly. The downswing is a purely reflex action from this position.

The other area in which women could improve their golf is on the putting green, and if they would spend only 15 minutes a week practicing that part of their game their scores would tumble dramatically. Watching a woman player with a good technique, who can play a round of golf using just timing and rhythm, is a joy.

Bottom row *When viewed from the front the rotation of the arms and clubface through the hitting area can be seen △. Also apparent is the way the woman golfer has kept her body upright, which has allowed her arms a free swing through the ball △. This is an important factor in enabling her to keep the club swinging to the end of her long follow-through △. The upright body position also makes it easy to transfer all the weight on to the left leg △.*

Australian Jan Stephenson, now a regular competitor on the United States LPGA Tour, is supple enough to achieve a very full and long follow-through.

3 PLAYING WOODS AND IRONS

Golf is a target game played over a variety of terrain. Each club in the golf bag is designed for a specific purpose – that is, to hit the ball over different distances and at different trajectories. Although the basic swing remains the same, certain adjustments have to be made according to whether the player is using a driver, a fairway wood, a long iron, a medium iron or a short iron. To become a complete golfer, you must be aware of the different consequences resulting from the use of each of these clubs.

▶ TARGET ◀

To show how different clubs produce shots of different length and trajectory.

ACHIEVEMENT

Knowledge of each club's capacity and therefore confidence in controlling the ball without having to make unnecessary adjustments to swing technique.

Jack Nicklaus

Fuzzy Zoeller tees off at Turnberry's 9th hole during the 1986 Open Championship. Zoeller is a powerful player and therefore, in the interests of accuracy, is hitting an iron club from the tee instead of a wood. It is not mandatory that the tee shot on a long hole is hit with a wood, very often an iron shot will keep the ball in play and make par figures more realistic.

THE DRIVER

In Chapter 2 we looked at the full swing. Now we will look at the shots that can be produced with it. The first shot in golf is the drive, and that is where we will begin.

The first thing to say about the drive is that it is probably the easiest shot in golf in that you are standing on level ground, you can decide from which part of the tee you want to play, the ball is sitting up waiting to be hit, and the fairway is the largest target you have on the golf course. Driving is difficult, however, because most of the time you are trying to hit the ball as far as you can. This means that you are exposing your swing to maximum pressure. In addition, the driver has the straightest face of all the golf clubs and, because you hit the ball on its "equator," the straight face allows you to impose sidespin on the ball far more easily than you could impose backspin. (To produce backspin you have to hit the ball at the "bottom.") Therefore, although the conditions in which you start are the best you can give yourself, the demands of the shot probably put the player under as much pressure as anything else on the golf course. It is tempting to let your physical strength overpower your golfing technique because you are trying to hit the ball as far as you can. This is folly: to produce distance you must swing the club as fast as you can, and you cannot move the club any faster than you can swing it.

⚠ *Because the ball is teed above the ground, at address it should be positioned more toward the left foot. This is so the ball can be struck at a point in the arc where the club is starting to swing up. Striking the ball on the upswing gives the shot less backspin and therefore more forward momentum.*

TEE HEIGHT

The first practical question is, how high do you tee the ball? The minimum height at which the ball must be teed is that at which half of it is visible above the crown of the driver. The crown is the top of the driver's head. This allows you

Inset *The correct way to tee the ball is to push the tee in the ground so that half the ball is visible above the top of the driver.*

52

⚠ The effect of having the ball teed up and further forward in the stance allows the player to sweep the club back more around the body, forcing the right elbow closer to the side.

⚠ Swinging the club around the body in this manner increases the shoulder turn and coils the left side to the maximum.

2

3

Viewed from behind it is clear that the club has been swung around the body and the weight has been transferred on to the right leg ▷₂. The body is fully turned behind the ball ▷₃.

2

1

3

As the club approaches the ball in the downswing the pull of the hips is apparent. The toe of the club points up in the air before being squared up at impact by the uncocking of the wrists. The right elbow is close to the body, indicating that the hit will be made from inside the target line ▷4▷. At impact the hips have continued to turn to the left and the uncocking of the wrists has squared up the clubface ▷5▷.

The correct finish to the swing has the player in a relaxed position, his left side straight and his hips and shoulders horizontal to the ground ▷6▷.

Viewed from the front it is evident that the body has stayed behind the ball, thereby allowing the player to strike the ball squarely in the back $\triangle$, $\triangle$. The body should not be allowed to straighten until after impact, and at the finish of the swing the body is erect and facing the target $\triangle$. This finish can be achieved only by the correct rotation of the hands and arms through the ball.

to sweep the ball up into the air and increase the effective loft on the club when you are hitting. You are trying to drive the ball a long way; so you want to eliminate as much backspin as possible. By teeing the ball up into the air, you are able to hit up behind it and hit slightly over the ball to minimize the backspin. Moreover, by teeing the ball high, you are able to move it further to the left in your stance, thereby allowing yourself more downswing to use to strike the ball. Modern drivers have 12 degrees angle of loft on the clubface. In the old days, drivers were made with 8 or 9 degrees of loft on the face, and it was therefore important to tee the ball up high so that you could add to the effective loft by driving the ball up into the air. You are going for maximum distance, and the desire to overpower the shot is great: you have to discipline yourself to create the same technique for the driver that you learned in the previous chapter.

Driving is golf's offensive shot. It is a shot that, provided it is played properly, completes approximately half the hole in perfect position. A first-rate shot with a driver on a par 4 leaves the shortest possible club to play for the second shot and, on a par 5, often brings the green within range of the second shot.

Many golfers are frightened to hit with a number 1 wood, and they prefer to take their chances with a 2, or even these days a 3, wood from the tee. This is taking away one of the great joys of the game. To see a properly driven ball hanging up in the air, traveling forward as far as you know you can hit it out of the middle of the club is one of the great thrills of golf.

The idea of hitting a 3 wood and leaving the ball in play is all very well for the top tournament professional, who is quite capable of hitting a driver but has picked the part of the fairway he wants the ball to land. For the average golfer, that is just laziness, because he has not bothered to develop the skill to play the game properly.

When you watch the great drivers such as Jack Nicklaus, Greg Norman or Ian Woosnam, and you see the prodigious distances that they drive the ball, you can understand how they bring in scores in the low and middle 60s. This is the one skill in golf that distinguishes the great tournament professionals from the top-class amateurs. Very few amateurs develop their golfing muscles to the point that they can generate the speed that these great players can. Norman, particularly, is one of the longest straight hitters of all time.

Apart from the wedges and the putter, the driver is the most frequently used club in the bag. Therefore, it makes good sense to find a driver that you like, and that you feel you can use and make a friend of.

It is far easier to follow through with the driver than it is with any of the other clubs in the bag because the ball is teed up. You are striking the ball with the club already swinging up toward the follow-through, and you are using maximum power. Therefore, the momentum of the club will make the follow-through longer, and at the end of the swing the shaft of the driver will be lying across your shoulders behind you.

FAIRWAY WOODS

The fairway woods are numbers 3, 4 and 5, and the difference in distance between is only about 12 yards a club. The technique for using the fairway woods differs from the technique for the driver in that the ball is sitting on the ground and you have to sweep the ball forward and off the turf to make it fly. A shot with the 3 wood is therefore the most dangerous shot in golf because it has the least amount of loft on it necessary to make the ball fly up into the air. The lie in which you find the ball before you play your 3 wood is critical. If the ground is very bare and the lie very tight, or if the opposite occurs, and the ball lies cupped in the grass, it is better not to play the 3 wood at all, but to consider the 4 or 5 woods, which have more loft and will elevate the ball more quickly

The 4 wood is a good club to use from the fairway or from a good lie in the semi-rough; the 5 wood is a good club to use from semi-rough or for any shots that require a high trajectory, perhaps over bunkers or over water, into the green from around the 200 yards mark. With both the 4 and 5 woods the sweeping action of the club through the ball elevates it into the air. You must not try to lift the ball into the air with these clubs; you will end up topping the ball if you do. If anything, the ball should be struck with a slightly downward blow, in the same way that you would strike down slightly on the long irons.

Many tournament players use the 3 wood from the tee to obtain extra control. Sometimes, when they are laying

Top row The shorter shaft of the fairway wood creates a slightly more upright swing plane, which makes it easier for the player to hit the ball into the air ▷. The wide sole on the bottom of the fairway wood allows the ball to be played further back in stance without fear of the clubhead digging into the ground ▷.

2

3

Bottom row The fairway wood shot is the longest shot to be played off the ground. The ball should be positioned more toward the center of the stance △ than with the driver as the club should be at the bottom of its arc when it makes contact with the ball. Because the fairway wood is slightly shorter than the driver, the player will stand closer to the ball △ .

up on a very narrow hole, the extra backspin that is generated by the more lofted 3 wood will keep the ball straighter than the same shot with a driver and they are prepared to sacrifice 15-20 yards distance from the driver shot for the extra control they get with a 3 wood.

When playing the 3 wood from the tee, the ball should be teed just on top of the grass to duplicate the sort of situation that would obtain if the ball were in the perfect lie on the fairway. This way, the approach to the shot can be the same as it would be out of the fairway – that is, it should be possible to sweep the ball forward off the top of the turf rather than either swinging up at it if the ball were teed up too high or having to chop down on it if the ball were down in the grass.

The 4 and 5 woods can be played from the tee on long par 4 holes, and it is possible to recreate a good lie on the turf with them as well. Therefore, you should tee the ball just on top of the grass and sweep the ball forward off it when you swing.

The 6 and 7 woods have become popular over the last few years, particularly with women golfers and men who are not strong enough to handle the long irons. These clubs are played in exactly the same way as the 4 and 5 woods. They are popular because they will guarantee the trajectory that a long iron will not if you want to play a high dropping, stopping shot from 170-190 yards. You will be able to sweep the ball away more successfully with a wood than punch it with an iron, which gives a high, arching shot while the iron is driven forward lower.

However, whichever club is used, there should be no change in swing technique. The club should be swung away from the ball with the left arm and hand, while the left shoulder is pulled around, stretching the muscles in the left side until they are so tight that the left hip is forced to turn a little too. The weight is transferred on to the right leg in the backswing, and the downswing is started by turning the left hip to the left and maintaining, or even tightening, the stretched left side a little more and pulling the club through the ball with the left arm to the end of the follow-through. The accent throughout is on pulling the club forward.

When you are using the fairway woods, the ball should be positioned half-way between the left heel and the center of the stance.

Right *The temptation to scoop the ball into the air must be resisted ⚠. The lie of the ball must be carefully assessed before the player selects the correct fairway wood. The tighter the ball is lying to the ground, the more lofted the club should be.*

Above *The rear view of the fairway wood shot is exactly the same as that of the driver ▷ except that the ball is positioned further back in the stance and struck at the bottom of the arc ▷. Fairway woods should be used only when the ball is sitting up reasonably well on the grass.*

Above Because the club meets the ball at the bottom of the swing arc, the extra loft will impart more backspin and guarantee a higher trajectory to the shot △6 . The average golfer usually finds long irons difficult to play and prefers to use a fairway wood. For this reason, 6 and 7 woods have enjoyed increased popularity. The technique for playing these is exactly the same as for the longer fairway woods.

59

IRON SHOTS

In a normal set of 14 clubs, which is all that you are allowed under the Rules of Golf, golfers tend to carry three wooden clubs and a putter. This means that the maximum number of irons that can be used is 10, which are normally the 2, 3, 4, 5, 6, 7, 8, 9 and the pitching wedge and sand wedge. Some people, however, prefer to add a third wedge, usually a more lofted wedge, of 60 degrees, in place of a 2 iron, which for many amateurs is extremely difficult to hit well constantly. A lot of amateurs opt for a fourth wood instead of either an extra wedge or a 2 iron.

The ball is played just forward of the center of the stance because it is vital that the hands are ahead of the blade, both at address and at impact. Increasing the amount that you push your hands forward increases the amount of backspin that can be imparted to the golf ball. Irons are the clubs that give the greatest accuracy; therefore, the more backspin you can impart to the ball when you strike it with an iron, the straighter the ball is going to fly, and the backspin helps when the ball lands.

LENGTH OF SHAFT

As the numbers on the irons get higher, the shaft gets shorter; this means that with the higher number irons, you have to stand a little closer to the ball. Again this helps you to hit down on the ball and create the backspin that is so necessary on these shots. You have to stand closer to the ball and, without having to do anything else, your swing

A full set of irons comprises nine clubs. They are the 3, 4, 5, 6, 7, 8 and 9, the pitching wedge and sand iron. The 3 iron has the least amount of loft on the face and the sand iron the most. The 3 iron is the longest club and the pitching wedge and the sand iron the shortest. The differences between each club is about four degrees in loft and 1/2 inches in length. Additions to the standard set are the 1 and 2 irons and a 60 degree wedge. The distances achieved with each club will depend on the player's ability, but the difference between each club should be constant.

automatically becomes more upright. This is a result of the shorter shaft, not of any conscious alteration in your swing technique. Because you are looking for accuracy, you do not have to hit the ball as hard as you possibly can, only sufficiently hard to make it travel the distance you require. One of the keys to consistent iron play is to keep the tempo smooth; if you hit a 6 iron 160 yards, you should hit every 6 iron 160 yards. If you have to hit the ball 170 yards you need to use a 5 iron, not to take a harder swing with the 6.

The shafts of the irons are shorter than those of the woods, and you may find that when you keep your hands leading as you go through the ball, you shave the grass with the club as it keeps descending to the bottom of its arc after you have hit the ball. This is a good sign, and is an excellent

way of checking whether your club is swinging toward the target or not. After you have hit the ball, stand behind the divot and look to see which way it points. It should point either toward the target or very slightly to the left of it. A divot that points to the right of the target is no good to anyone and means that the shot has been pushed.

SHORT IRONS

When you are playing the high-numbered irons, numbers 7, 8 and 9 or the wedges, you are looking for so much accuracy that you do not really want to make a full swing. A three-quarter swing, keeping your rhythm, will give you the accuracy that you require. Remember, when you use iron shots, you are looking for accuracy, not power. In addition, because the shafts are shorter with these clubs,

the divot will be deepest. No divot should ever be much more than a quarter of an inch into the ground but it will always be most noticeable after you have struck the ball with these clubs. When you are playing iron shots, pull the club through the ball toward the target. Always keep the target in mind and always make sure that your swing goes toward it. Then, even a ball that is not hit exactly in the middle of the club, will fly in that direction.

LONG IRONS

Long irons are the most difficult clubs to use because they require the same sort of technique that is used with the fairway woods. You must make a good hard swing at the ball and have a long follow-through, pulling the club toward the target along the way. Long irons are difficult to play because they lack the loft of the other irons; therefore, the amount of backspin imparted to the ball is less and the ball does not rise into the air as easily as it would with, say, a 4 or 5 iron. In addition, because less backspin is imparted to the ball, the chances of getting sidespin increase, and it is not as easy to hit the ball straight with a long iron as it is with a middle iron.

However, if you practice hard and keep on pulling the club through toward the target whenever you play, you'll soon become a proficient long-iron player.

These days many top tournament golfers prefer to hit a 1 iron from the tee than play a driver on very tight holes or holes that do not need the full distance from the tee. They hit a 1 iron because the shorter shaft gives them greater control over the ball, and a 1 iron has 6 or 7 degrees more loft than a driver. It is consequently easier to control a straight shot because of the extra backspin that is imparted, and top players can usually hit the ball with a 1 iron within 15-20 yards of their longest drive. Although the 1 iron and the 3 wood have a similar amount of loft, the 1 iron, with its shorter shaft, tends to be driven forward on a lower trajectory with more backspin, while the 3 wood tends to be swept into the air, where it is more vulnerable to the wind and the elements.

The irons are the scoring clubs in golf. Any player who hits irons well will find more greens with his second shots.

THE 2 IRON AT ADDRESS

Right The technique required to play a 2 iron is the same as for a fairway wood. The ball should be positioned just to the left of the center of the stance to ensure that it is struck at the bottom of the swing arc. The shaft in the 2 iron is shorter than that of the 3 wood, which allows the player to swing in a slightly more upright plane.

Inset The loft of the club produces a climbing, soaring shot, which stops more quickly than a fairway wood shot.

62

THE 6 IRON AT ADDRESS

Below The 6 iron is 2 inches shorter than the 2 iron and is designed for accuracy. This club should never be used for maximum distance as control is paramount. The ball position is, again, at the bottom of the swing arc.

Inset Because the club shows plenty of loft to the player, the temptation is not to scoop the ball into the air but to chop down on it. This action negates the loft and produces an incorrect lower trajectory.

THE WEDGE AT ADDRESS

Below The wedge is designed totally for accuracy and distance should never be a factor. It should never be used from more than 100 yards from the target. The technique required is usually less than a full swing, which means the shoulders turn but the movement of the lower body is restricted.

Inset The loft on the wedge enables the ball to be hit at a much higher trajectory.

THE 2-IRON SWING

A perfectly played 2 iron can provide one of the greatest pleasures in golf. Because of its lack of loft a 2-iron shot should only be attempted from the fairway but with a sound swing technique this club can soon be mastered.

◁ The technique for the 2 iron is a balanced address position with the hands slightly ahead of the ball.

▷ The takeaway is initiated by the left arm and shoulder turning over the right leg.

3 *At the top of the backswing the weight is coiled on the right side of the body. The hips have turned only a minimum amount and the left heel is slightly off the ground.*

4 *The unwinding of the hips is started by transferring the weight on to the left leg.*

⚠️ 5 Approaching impact, the hips are continuing to unwind and the weight is now almost totally transferred on to the left leg.

⚠️ 6 The head is behind the ball to enable the golfer to swing away from himself and toward the target. At shoulder height in the follow-through the hips have turned as far as they can, and the hands have released the clubface in plane through the ball.

5

6

⚠ At the end of the swing the weight is totally on the left leg and the right foot, which bears no weight, is balanced on the toe.

GREG NORMAN

Because of his great length Greg Norman can attack any course he plays, which suits his confident Australian nature. Although his game is based on power, Norman is a fine short game player and a particularly good putter. He is a superb player, who has worked hard at his game and continues to do so.

Greg Norman, a consummate long-iron player, at the top of his swing. This most powerful player has made a huge shoulder turn in order to create the power he needs to execute this shot.

THE 6-IRON SWING

The 6 iron is the classic middle-iron club. Most golfers are confident with a 6 iron because it is usually the club they learn to play with when they start. It has a fair amount of loft but not too much and gives a satisfactory flight to the ball.

⚠ *At address the shorter shaft on the 6 iron requires that the player bends over a little more from the waist.*

⚠ *This means that the club is taken back straighter along the target line and less around the body.*

⚠3 *This is a result of the shorter shaft and should not be a conscious move on the part of the player.*

⚠4 *As this is an accuracy club, rhythm and tempo are of prime importance, and the weight shift on the backswing will act as governor on the pace of the swing.*

△ The start of the downswing should not be hurried. The weight should be transferred smoothly on to the left leg, and this will set up a chain reaction which will pull the club through the ball in a rhythmic manner.

△ The follow-through will not be as long because the club has not been swung so fast.

⚠ Therefore, it should be easier to maintain balance at the finish. The essence of a 6-iron shot is to hit the ball a particular distance and direction without undue effort.

IAN WOOSNAM

Ian Woosnam has reaped the benefits of hard work on the practice tee perfecting possibly the most simple method used by any of today's top stars. Although only 5 feet 5 inches tall, Woosnam's swing is quite upright because he swings the club straight back from the ball. This allows his shoulders to turn fully while restricting his hip turn to a minimum. He has very strong hands and arms and is able to hit the ball very hard without seeming to apply much effort. This easy rhythm is what makes Woosnam's swing look so simple.

Ian Woosnam at the top of the swing with a 6 iron.

USING A WEDGE

After the putter, the wedge is used more than any other club in the bag; practice with this club is therefore important. The shorter shaft and extra loft are designed to promote accuracy, and power is not required.

⚠ *When the wedge is used, the stance to the ball is closer because of the shorter shaft, and this creates a more upright swing plane. The weight is equally balanced on both feet.*

⚠ *The swing commences when the weight is shifted onto the right leg. The club is swung back by the turn of the shoulders, and there is no independent hand action. The right arm is folded close into the right side.*

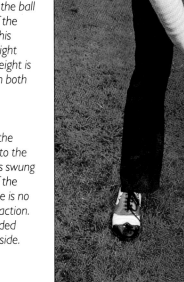

3. Because accuracy is required and the swing plane is more upright, there is less body turn and more arm swing. The wrists are kept firm, and the backswing is a little shorter than it would be if full power were required.

The body is perfectly balanced behind the ball, with the weight on the right leg while the left heel remains in contact with the ground.

4. The downswing is initiated by the left hip turning to the left and thereby transferring the weight to the left foot. This stretches the muscle between the left hip and left shoulder and means that the hips are ahead of the shoulders. The wrists are still fully cocked, which keeps the right arm close to the right side. The head is behind the ball, and the initial unwinding of the hips has started to draw the right heel from the ground.

⚠️ *At impact the body is balanced on the left foot, and the hands, which are pulling the club, are ahead of the ball. The left hip is still turning to the left, and the right leg is thrusting toward the target, which allows the club to be* swung and held on the target line longer. This is the great advantage of having a wide stance. The hands leading in this manner will ensure that the ball is struck before the turf.

⚠️ *After the ball has been struck, the club continues to move toward the target. When the wedge is used, the hands do not cross over as early in the follow-through, which creates a wider arc through the ball. This is* essential for accuracy. The weight is now totally on the left leg, and the head is just starting to come up as the body is straightening.

⚠ At the finish of the swing the left side is straight and the hips and shoulders are level with the ground. The right foot rests vertically on the toe and, because no power has been put into the swing, the club has not swung past the head in the follow-through.

TOM WEISKOPF

Tom Weiskopf had the most natural, elegant, powerful swing of any of the top professionals competing over the last 25 years. British Open Champion in 1973, his successes were limited because of his fiery temperament. There was no more awe-inspiring sight in golf than Weiskopf playing well but a poor bounce, a slight mishit would ruin the hole, the round and, sometimes, the day. His swing was long, free and powerful.

Above Tom Weiskopf demonstrates the classic top-of-the-swing position with a wedge. He has achieved this position by turning his shoulders and restricting his hip movement.

Right *High-speed photography reveals the moment of truth when an iron strikes a golf ball. The amount the ball is compressed is dictated by the speed at which the club strikes it, but the primary effect of an iron shot is the backspin put on the ball. Backspin provides control over the shot and creates a straighter flight. When the ball is compressed between the grooves on the club and the grass, backspin is created to provide aerodynamic efficiency. Golf balls are made in three types of compression – 80, 90 and 100. Compression will vary according to the type of ball used: the softer the ball (80) the easier it is to compress. The cover and construction of the ball also affects backspin velocity. Two-piece Surlyn-covered balls leave the clubface at approximately 7,000 revolutions per minute while a wound, Balata-covered ball will leave the clubface at 9,000 rpm.*

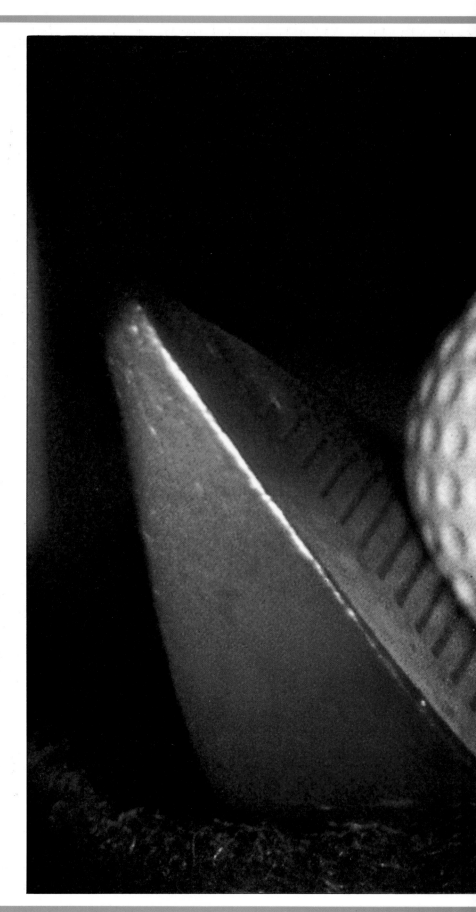

4 MASTERING THE SHORT GAME

While the thrill of golf is encapsulated in the sight of a well-struck drive, the essence of good scoring lies in the short game. These are the shots played from within 100 yards of the flagstick, and proficiency in this department will reap swift rewards, simply because shots from this distance are required more frequently than any others. In this chapter we will discuss the three basic shots that are made in this area depending on the distance the player is from the flag, and also explain how to recover effectively from bunkers.

TARGET

To provide a full range of recovery shots which are vital if the lowest score is to be produced.

ACHIEVEMENT

Confidence that a good short game will always make up for any inadequacies in the long game.

Gordon Brand Junior

Paul Way hits a pitch shot
and produces a shower
of earth in the process.
The ball will have been
squeezed between the
clubface and the turf
thereby producing
backspin which, in turn,
keeps the ball on line
during its flight. Notice
how Way is still looking
at the spot where the
ball was and how his left
wrist has not collapsed
with the impact.

THE CHIP SHOT

When you are chipping you want the ball to roll as much as possible because the rolling ball has more chance of going into the hole. You need to conceive a shot that flies as low as possible before it hits the ground. Therefore, most chip shots are played within 5 yards of the edge of the green. As you want minimum flight and maximum roll, this shot should be played with a 5, 6 or 7 iron and the technique is described below.

Stand close to the ball and try to get your eyes as nearly over the top of the ball as you can. Hold the club at the bottom of the grip to give maximum control of the club. You should use the same grip for the short game as you would for the long, although some very good chippers see this part of the game as an extension of the putting stroke and use their putting grip on these shots. Because you are trying to get your eyes as nearly over the top of the ball as you can and you are gripping the club down at the bottom of the grip, you will bend over the shot more than you would if you were playing a full 5 iron shot. Then, with the weight of your body balanced toward the balls of the feet and with your head over the ball, your stance – the line through the feet, the hips and the shoulders – should be at right angles to the line you are trying to hit along. Your arms should be close to your body and your feet should be close together, no more than 6 inches apart.

You should make sure that the sole of the club lies flat on the ground so that the ball is hit in the direction you want it to go. If the toe of the club is on the ground and the heel of the club off it, the ball would be despatched to the right of the target; conversely, if the heel was on the ground and the toe up in the air, the ball would be pulled to the left of the target.

DEVELOPING A FIRM-WRISTED STROKE

The most important thing about the technique of playing the chip shot is that the wrists must be kept firm throughout the stroke. Place your hands slightly ahead of the ball, as with all the other shots, and then, during the backswing, keep your wrists firm and swing the club low to the ground, using your arms and shoulders. Keep your body as still as possible, moving only to accommodate the slight rock of your shoulders as the club is swung backwards. The through swing should just be as long as the backswing to keep the tempo of the swing smooth. You do not require any wristwork in the swing for a chip shot because the wrists create swing speed and acceleration, and a chip shot does not require great speed, only consistency. Keeping the wrists firm allows you to control the speed of the club head far more efficiently than if you were to introduce wrist action. The other reason for eliminating wrist action from the shot is that cocking the wrists causes the club to swing in quite a sharp arc, and the clubhead would come up off the ground in the backswing, making it very easy, if the downswing were slightly mistimed, to hit the shot inaccurately. A wristless stroke keeps the club at ground level far longer.

In the address position for the chip shot the ball is placed opposite the inside of the left heel. The hands are in front of the clubface and the weight favors the left foot △. The backswing is created by rocking the shoulders to ensure that the stroke is played with the arms, not with the wrists. This method keeps the clubface pointing toward the target △. At impact, the arms have swung back toward the target, allowing the clubface to dispatch the ball in the intended direction. The body has been kept perfectly still throughout △.

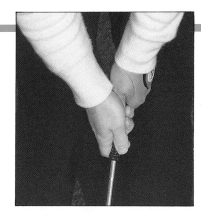

Above *For accuracy and control the club should be held at the bottom of the grip.*

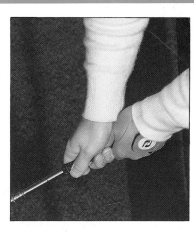

Above *Gripping the club in this way helps to keep the wrists firm throughout the stroke.*

Below *At impact, the hands mirror the address position.*

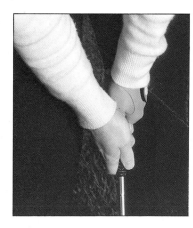

2

3

Viewed from behind, the address position shows the head over the ball and the body bent forward more because the club has been held short .

At the top of the backswing, the club has been swung directly away from the target by the arms while the body is kept perfectly still .

Because the weight is on the left foot at address, the club will be slightly on the downswing when it catches the ball before the turf △₃.

The head will have remained in the same position throughout the stroke, which allows the club to swing toward the hole ▷.

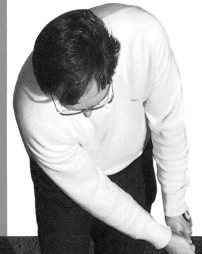

The length of the follow-through is the same as the length of the backswing. The head and body have remained still as the arms have swung through △₄.

Inset Because the stroke has been played with the arms, the hands and club do not turn over in the follow-through.

HOW LOFT GOVERNS TRAJECTORY

The trajectory of shots toward the flag will be governed by the loft of the club used. The chip shot produces a low trajectory with maximum roll. The pitch and run produces a higher trajectory with a matching amount of roll. The pitch shot produces maximum trajectory, which causes the ball to drop so steeply that there is little or no forward momentum when it lands.

4

If you are attempting a chip shot from just off the edge of the green, try to duplicate your putting stroke as nearly as you can because it is far easier to judge distance and line when you are thinking of the shot in terms of the putt than it is to try to produce the same shot by thinking of it as some sort of low percentage of your full swing.

When you are playing a chip shot, the ball should be played from the middle of your stance. This makes it easier for you to keep your hands ahead of the ball both at address and at impact.

SELECTING A CLUB

The clubs used for the shot should be selected to keep the ball in the air long enough to make sure it lands on the smooth cut of the green. Generally, the clubs with straighter faces are more likely to do an efficient job of rolling the ball accurately. A shot that lands on the fringe of the green might bounce anywhere. Do not try to scoop the ball up into the air, for the loft on the club will do that if you allow it to swing through the ball toward the target. If your ball were on the putting green, you would refuse a 5 iron because the ball would fly up into the air before it started to roll. This is exactly what a chip shot is. A putting stroke with a lofted club.

6 iron

9 iron

Pitching wedge

THE PITCH-AND-RUN SHOT

A pitch-and-run shot requires almost the same technique as the chip. The difference is that the ball would be further back from the green, probably between 5 and 20 yards further back, and the clubs used would be the 7, 8 or 9 iron. The stance would be a little wider and again the head should be as near over the ball as it could possibly be placed. The hands should be close to the body for control, and the weight should be evenly balanced on both feet. The ball is played in the center of the stance, and again the shot is played just with the arms and shoulders: the wrists are not used. The backswing would be a little longer, probably going back to between knee and hip height, and the follow-through should be the same length as the backswing because you do not want to hit at the ball quickly or jab at it. It is important to keep the tempo of the swing smooth. The extra loft on the 7, 8 and 9 irons means that the trajectory of the ball will be higher.

Top row In the address position, the hands are ahead of the ball, the weight favors the left foot, and the head is behind the ball △.
The club has been swung straight back from the ball and away from the target using just the arms. The backswing is generous because sudden acceleration, which creates backspin, is not needed on this shot △.
Body movement has been kept to a minimum △.
The club has continued to swing toward the target with the hands continuing to lead the clubface △.

1

2

2

3

4

3

4

87

Bottom row *Viewed from behind, the hands are close to the body to allow the head to be over the ball. This makes lining up the shot considerably easier* ▷.
Because the arms swing back without any wrist action, the clubface can be kept pointing toward the target, which will guarantee a straight shot as long as the body is kept still ▷.
At impact, the position of the body reflects the address position ▷. *The club continues to swing through the ball toward the target, pulling the right shoulder underneath the stationary head. It is vital that the follow-through should be at least as long as the backswing.* ▷.

THE PITCH SHOT

If you use the same method for the chip and the pitch-and-run shots but play with a pitching wedge or a sand wedge, you will have a pitch shot. A pitch shot climbs steeply into the air, drops almost vertically on to the green with backspin and settles near to the point where it lands. The shot is played with just the arms and shoulders; the wrists are not used. You will find that the maximum distance for this shot without any wrist action is around 40-50 yards. When you come to want to hit the ball further than this, you have to introduce some wrist action to get the clubhead swinging more quickly; wrist action should not be introduced into the shot until you are swinging at maximum length with your arms and shoulders. This will be at a point where your hands are swinging up to about shoulder height.

When you are playing an ordinary pitch shot it is vital that the follow-through be at least as long as the backswing, because the follow-through allows the club to use its natural loft to get the ball up into the air. The stance should alter slightly and become slightly open: a line through the feet will point to the left of the target. This is to encourage you to slice slightly across the ball to make the ball fly higher and spin a little more. The last thing you want when you are playing the wedges is a pull or a hook. A slightly open stance allows the club to be swung a little way outside the target line in the takeaway and across that same target line in the downswing, which imparts a slight left-to-right spin to the ball and helps to make the ball climb and land more softly.

THE 60 DEGREE WEDGE

An important addition to the modern short game has been the introduction of the 60 degree wedge, which should be played in exactly the same way as the others – that is, with arm and shoulder, not wrist, action. This club has come into use because the modern professionals have evolved a

⚠ At address the most important thing is to have the hands ahead of the ball so that it can be struck a downward blow.

⚠ At the top of the backswing, less weight is transferred on to the right foot because the backswing has been made by swinging the arms up.

⚠ Although the weight is on the left side, the head is still behind the ball.

⚠ At the end of the swing the clubface has deliberately been held open in order to give the shot maximum height.

88

method that includes only arm and shoulder action in their short game swing. If you try to play a 60 degree wedge and flick your wrists, you will hit underneath the ball, and will never get the ball to travel a consistent distance because the angle is just too great. Played with no wrist action, the loft of the club can be used effectively both from the fairway and out of the rough and out of bunkers. This club has so much loft on it that to open the clubface and increase that loft makes it impossible to move the ball forward at all.

Many amateurs watch the professionals on television playing pitch shots that spin the ball back huge distances on the green, and they wonder how they can add this shot to their own game. In fact, the professionals do nothing different from the amateurs: they just do it better. They strike the ball more solidly with the pitching clubs, swing the clubs forward to strike the bottom of the ball and allow the natural loft of the club to spin the ball up in the air. It is the quality of the strike that produces this backspin, not a trick that the professional keeps up his sleeve. To produce this backspin the hands must be ahead of the ball at impact and the club must be accelerating into the ball.

Even the professionals get this sort of backspin only when they are playing a reasonably full shot. They cannot produce it if they are not hitting the ball hard. Many amateurs try to play shots from 20 or 30 yards and expect to get the same amount of backspin that the professionals get when they are hitting the ball 80 or 90 yards. It is important to remember that if you use a shot that produces so much backspin, you must pitch the ball behind the hole for it to finish close to the hole. This makes courses that are already far too long for the average amateur play even longer. It is much more sensible for amateurs to play a pitch shot that they know will settle or perhaps run a few feet forward rather than try to dig the ball in and make it spin back all the time.

Inset *When the ball hits the green from a pitch shot it usually leaves an indentation known as a "ball mark," in the green. It is common courtesy, and within the rules of the game, to repair the damage.*

SAND PLAY

There never has been nor will there ever be a golfer who can hit the ball absolutely straight on target all the time. Everybody at some time finds himself hacking the ball out of the rough, bending it around, under or over trees, and blasting it out of bunkers. The sooner you learn how to recover from these situations, in a way that doesn't damage your score too much, the better golfer you are going to be.

When your ball is lying in a bunker, your first thought should be to get it out in one shot first time. How close you can get it to your target is of secondary importance. The first rule of trouble play is that if you have one trouble shot, you shouldn't leave yourself another for your next shot. Shortly after the war, some teachers seemed to believe that by trivializing the technique for playing out of bunkers, they made it easy for the pupil to recover. They used to say that the bunker shot was the easiest shot in golf because you didn't have to hit the ball. While this is perfectly true, you did have to hit the sand, and judging the texture, firmness and wetness of the sand is quite a chore in itself, certainly more difficult than simply trying to hit a golf ball. Because you are trying to hit the sand dictates how you should address the ball.

The Rules of Golf do not allow you to place your club on the sand behind the ball; you have to keep it above the ball until you strike it. However, the rules do allow you to wriggle your feet in the sand to help you to judge the texture of the sand, to allow you to establish a good firm foothold in loose sand, and to lower you down so that your swing path will be a little more under the ball.

You should play the ball forward in the stance just inside the left heel, but on short bunker shots your stance is aimed about 10 feet left of the hole. When you address the ball, you should open the clubface so that, rather than pointing 10 feet left of the hole, it points at the hole so that it is opened up in relation to the line you are going to swing along. Your hands must still obey the first rule of golf: they must be ahead of the ball and of the clubface. Your hips and shoulders will be a little open because the ball is forward in your stance.

The sand wedge has a thick flange on the bottom of it, and the back of the flange trails somewhat below the front so that when you swing into the sand, the back of the flange makes contact first to ensure that the club runs through the top of the sand rather than digging in and getting stuck somewhere beneath the ball. You want the club to run through the top of the sand; you do not want it to dig in an

Below left *The differences between the sand wedge and the pitching wedge are about 5 degrees of loft and considerably more bounce on the sole. Bounce is the* amount by which the back of the sole of the club is lower than the front. Sand wedges, therefore, have a wider sole than pitching wedges.

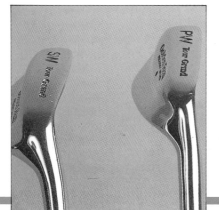

Left *The rules do not allow the player to touch the sand with the club before the swing is made; therefore the ball has to be addressed with the club above it.*

To play a sand shot, the ball must be addressed opposite the left heel, and the feet should be slightly wider than for a pitch shot of the same length. The eye should be focused on the point in the sand at which the club should enter. The club is picked up steeply to eliminate the chances of scooping the ball out (1, 2, 3 **above** and **below**).

inch or more down below the ball. When you have wriggled your feet as you take your stance, you have established pretty much the texture of the first half inch of sand, and if your club runs through this top half inch of sand, rather than digging in below it, you will be working in conditions that you know. In addition, because the sand wedge will not be digging in, the amount of sand between the clubface and the ball when you strike is kept to the minimum, which means that you can relate the feel of the shot more closely to that of an ordinary pitch shot. By turning the clubface out toward the hole, you are increasing the effective loft of the club; so when you swing at the ball with the club cutting through the top of the sand and underneath the ball, the ball is going to shoot up in the air rather more quickly than it would in a pitch shot from grass. When it comes up so quickly, it drops quietly on the green with slice spin and will often run to the right.

The stance should be fairly wide to play a bunker shot: this lowers the body a little to reach the sand under the ball. It is important that you swing along the line of your feet –

that is, to the left of your target. This way you create the cutting spin that is essential to make the ball rise steeply out of the bunker, and, if you are playing a standard bunker shot where you don't want the ball to travel more than 30 or 40 feet the swing is pretty much the same as it would be if you were pitching from grass. The only difference is that you will make contact with the sand 2-2½inches behind the ball. Ordinary bunker shots do not need a lot of wrist action. This becomes necessary only when you need to dig further under the ball, if it is buried or lying in a heel mark.

As we have seen, the Rules of Golf do not allow you to ground your club behind the ball in the bunker. So you start the swing with the club hovering a hair above the sand. Then you swing in just the same way as if you were playing a normal pitch shot: swing backwards and down, and pull through with the left hand. Again, the important thing is to pull through. Because you are hitting the sand and not the ball, the tendency is to hit at the sand and then stop. The most important rule of playing sand shots is that you must follow through and pull the club through the sand. The sand runs up the face of the club so that when it makes contact with the face of the ball it acts like sandpaper and makes the ball spin sharply upwards. When the club carries on beyond the ball, do not let the hands cross over but keep the left hand in front of the blade and pulling through. At the end of the swing on a bunker shot of normal length, the club will finish up at about shoulder height with the face of the club pointing straight up in the air; it will not be turned over with the toe up as it would have been with a long shot.

The club should be swung firmly down into the sand behind the ball, so that the ball is "splashed" out of the bunker with the sand. It is important not to let the striking of the sand stop the club from swinging into the follow-through ▷ ⚠.

4

4

Certain adjustments have to be made in playing a long bunker shot from a shallow bunker. Check that the lip of the bunker is not so low that the ball will catch on it on the way out. From a shallow bunker it is possible to get good distance. Address the ball without grounding the club and play it just a little further to the right of your stance than you would normally do for the same club off the green. Hold the clubhead above the center of the ball; this will encourage you to make contact with the ball first △. The backswing should be the same as you would use for a normal shot △. Approaching impact the main objective is to pick the ball cleanly off the top of the sand △.

DEEP BUNKERS

Some greenside bunkers are extremely deep, and the ball has to be elevated very quickly from the sand. Do this merely by opening the clubface more and more. During bunker practice sessions it is a good idea to experiment and see how far you can open the clubface while still making the ball pop up in the air and go forward. Probably the greatest bunker shot ever played was one by Doug Sanders on the 71st hole of the British Open at St. Andrews in 1970. Sanders was leading the field by one shot coming down the 17th. His second shot on this par-4 hole drew just a little too sharply and rolled into the famous Road Bunker that sits greenside. From where he was standing close to the lip on the left of the bunker, Sanders opened the clubface an enormous amount and made his normal bunker shot swing. The result was the ball exploded out, high and soft, and finished within a foot of the cup.

Like all shots in the short game, bunker shots can be conquered with practice, but the one bunker shot that everyone dislikes is when the ball plugs into the sand and stays there; this is known as a "fried egg lie." To extricate yourself from this, play the ball a little further back, but not behind the center, in your stance and always to the left of center. Don't open the face of the club as much as you would if you were playing a ball on top of the sand, but aim straight at your target. When you swing, cock your wrists early in the backswing and lift the club up steeply. Very little body movement is needed on this shot. Just drop the club down firmly an inch behind the ball. The flange on the bottom of the club will prevent it from digging in too deeply and will allow the club to move forward and under the ball, which will come up out of the sand rather quickly after impact. The feeling is of chopping the club down into the sand behind the ball rather than of swinging forward through it. It doesn't matter in these circumstances if the club does not follow-through a long way as long as it goes past the ball.

SHALLOW BUNKERS

If you are playing from a shallow greenside bunker which doesn't have a lip on it, use your putter. The stroke is just the same as you would make on the putting green, except, of course, that you are not allowed to ground the club behind the ball before you play the shot. Remember that when you are putting through loose sand, the ball will not roll as quickly as it would on a tightly mown green; so you have to play the ball a little bit further than you would if it were on grass. If the bunker has only a slight lip to it and the ball is sitting nicely on top of the sand, chip the ball out. The technique is just the same as it would be for chipping from

The swing continues onto a normal finish ⁴ ⁵ ⁶ *but because the ball has been hit cleanly from the sand, greater backspin will* *have been imparted and the ball will land without much run.*

just off the edge of the green – hands forward, head still over the ball and the stroke played just with the arms and shoulders. This is a simple shot, although it has been considered more difficult than it actually is for years. The important point to remember about all bunker shots is that you are trying to get the ball up by hitting down and forward; you are never, ever trying to scoop the ball up.

If you play on a day when the sand is wet, you will find that its texture becomes thicker. If you are going to play a shot for which you would judge you have to hit dry sand 2 inches behind the ball, you will probably have to hit only one inch behind the ball to get almost exactly the same result in wet sand.

The secret of playing successful sand shots is to have a proper sand wedge. Anything else is just making the shot, which requires quite a lot of judgment, even more difficult. A sand wedge should have a big flange on it and a trailing edge that is lower than the front edge of the flange. If your

sand iron does not have a big flange on it, it will be difficult to get it to work on top of the sand: it will always dig in too much.

One final word about sand shots. When I see players in the sand bunkers trying to get out, they often try to play impossible shots. They try to hit the ball upwards and toward the target from the bottom of turf banks, when the sensible shot would be to come out sideways or even backwards from the bunker. There is no rule in golf that says that you must hit toward the flagstick. The first rule of sand shots is to get out first time in whatever direction you can guarantee recovery.

LONG BUNKER SHOTS
Occasionally you will drive into a fairway bunker, from which you may feel you can hit a long shot to the green. This shot is quite simple. Play the ball just a little further to the right in your stance than you would normally do for the

When the ball lies buried in a bunker several variations to normal bunker play are introduced. Because the ball is buried it is necessary to explode both the ball and the sand in which it is buried. The spin characteristics of the shot are different because the sand will prevent the club from slicing under the ball and thereby eliminate backspin and create topspin and more roll on the ball.

1

2

same club and make sure that your hands are slightly further in front of the blade than they would be on the normal shot. Then, focus your attention on the front of the ball, make your normal swing and you will find that you will hit the ball before you hit the sand. By focusing on the front of the ball and playing the ball a little further back, you can be sure of catching it earlier in your downswing arc. One word of warning when playing this shot: don't be greedy. If you feel you can reach the green with a 5 iron but the bank on the bunker might be in the way, take a 6 iron and play for the front edge. It is far better to finish up with a chip from the front edge of the green than it would be to be playing your third shot from within the bunker, after having hit the bank and toppled backwards.

When playing any bunker shot it is important that you keep your tempo smooth and don't try to hit too hard, which is always the temptation when you are trying to hit the sand rather than the ball.

The first thing the player has to do at address is reduce the amount of effective bounce on the sand wedge. This can be achieved by playing this shot with a pitching wedge or 9 iron, which has less bounce. Whichever club is used, however, the technique is the same. First, position the ball in the middle of the stance and close the clubface so that the club will be lifted straight up in the backswing △. From this position it is possible to drop the club straight down into the sand behind the ball, which is important as the club has to penetrate the sand to at least the height of the ball △.

3

On the downswing the body moves only enough to accommodate the downward swing of the arms, and the weight is planted on the left side △₃.

4

Because the direction of the blow has been so steeply downward, a long follow-through is impossible. This chopping action with a closed clubface brings the ball out on a low-running trajectory, and it is difficult to finesse the shot. The chief objective must be to get the ball out of the bunker with the first attempt △₄ △₅.

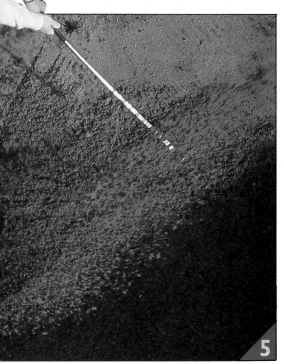

5

GARY PLAYER

Through long hours of practice as a young man, Gary Player made himself one of the finest bunker players in the world. Because he lacked the power of some of his contemporaries, he knew he would be hitting longer clubs to the green which would mean that he would miss more greens. So he taught himself to recover from bunkers in order to compete with his more powerful rivals. He became so good at recovery shots, it is said that on holes with difficult greens, Player would aim his second shot into the sand bunkers because he was more confident of getting his bunker shot close to the hole than he was a long putt. Player's ability to win in countries all over the world is in no small part due to his excellence when playing from sand. He is a great competitor who never gives up and this is typified in his attitude toward playing recovery shots.

5

PUTTING

Putting is often referred to as "the game within a game," and it is regarded in some quarters almost as an art form. In truth, putting is the easiest part of golf, simply because the ball is propelled along the ground for a relatively short distance and with a short swing. Becoming a consistently good putter requires no great athletic ability, only the adherence to certain fundamentals coupled with the development of judgment of distance in relation to the fall of the land.

▶ TARGET ◀

To understand that putting is half the game and that a good putter can compete with anyone.

ACHIEVEMENT

Good putting relieves the pressure on the rest of the game and a sound putting stroke can also capitalize on an accurate long game.

Ben Crenshaw

Hale Irwin holes a putt on the 13th green at Winged Foot during the 1984 United States Open Championship. Irwin is a very aggressive player and he is instinctively waving the putter to signal the ball into the hole.

HOLING OUT

Of all golf strokes, putting is the most personal. Individual styles vary dramatically among the best putters because they have found, after many long hours of practice on the putting green, the method that best works for them. The quickest way to improve your scores is to improve your putting. Psychologically, putting affects your long game. If you are holing out well there is less pressure on you to hit the ball close to the hole and you can relax. If you are putting badly you will feel that you have to hit the ball very close to the hole before you can make your putt, and this puts tremendous pressure on your game, which affects even the tee shot: you want to hit the ball in play off the tee to give yourself the best chance of hitting your second shot close to the hole because you don't feel you can make any long putts.

No single putting method is universally successful for everyone, but there are certain basic principles of the putting stroke to which all the great players adhere. If you have a putting method that works for you and with which you feel comfortable and confident, don't read any further in this chapter.

THE PUTTING GRIP

Now let's start with the putting grip. Putting is the stroke in golf that demands the greatest accuracy. So the first thing to do is align the putter's face so that it points along the path you want the ball to roll on. When you have aligned the blade toward the target, align your hands to it. As we have already stressed, the left hand is the master hand in all golf strokes, and if you place your left hand on the grip first, with your thumb directly on top of the club's shaft on the flat side of the grip (if your putter has a flat-sided grip), you will find that the back of the left hand points down the line you are trying to hit the ball along. If you point your fingers down you would find that the palm would be parallel to the putter's face.

When you add your right hand to the putter grip, place your right thumb on the top of the shaft just below the left. If you were to open your right hand, your fingers would point straight to the ground and your right palm would directly oppose your left. It would be parallel to the face of the putter. If you were to dispense with the putter altogether and roll the ball toward the hole, you would release the ball when your palm was facing the direction you wanted the ball to roll in. This is a natural alignment because your right palm and the clubface are pointing in the same direction. You can use the clubface as an extension of your right palm in finding the direction you want to roll the ball along. When your hands are in this position, you can control your putting stroke by thinking in terms of swinging either the back of the left hand or the palm of the right hand toward the hole.

Having got your hands at the right angle to the putter's blade, the next consideration is how to make contact with your grip on the club. Your thumbs should sit directly down the top of the shaft. This leaves the putter grip to be

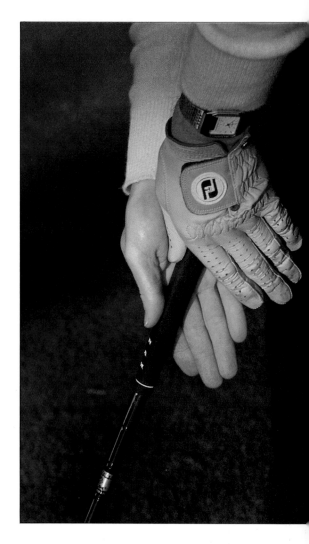

held in the fingers of both hands. Your thumbs are very sensitive, and by placing them down the top of the shaft you are able to transmit the amount of speed you need to the putter's head.

The hands can be joined in a variety of ways. The most popular putting grip is called the reverse overlap, in which the left forefinger is taken off the shaft and the right little finger slid back up the shaft so that it rests against the middle finger of the left hand. The left forefinger is then laid across the little finger or even down and across the last three fingers of the right hand. This gives more control of the stroke to the right hand. It is also possible to interlock the left forefinger and the right little finger on the shaft, and the conventional overlap grip should not be discarded if it feels comfortable. I prefer this conventional grip as it keeps the control of the putting stroke in the left hand. Some golfers overlap two fingers of their right hand over the fore- and middle fingers of the left hand, but this is just a matter of comfort. The most important thing about the

Building the grip for putting is made easier by the club manufacturers, who produce grips with flat tops. The flat surface of the grip is aligned at right angles to the blade and allows the hands to be placed on the grip in exactly the same way every time.

▷ The grip is built initially by placing both thumbs on the flat surface, and this means that the hands oppose each other exactly, with the back of the left hand and the palm of the right hand square to the putter blade.

▷ The next step is to curl the fingers of the right hand around the grip. All four fingers must be used as the right hand dominates the putting stroke.

▷ The grip is completed by folding the last three fingers of the left hand around the grip, with the forefinger of the left hand over-riding the fingers of the right. This grip, which is known as the reverse overlap grip is used by the vast majority of good putters and it increases the influences of the right hand on the grip and at the same time enables both hands to work as a single unit. It is important to eliminate excessive wrist action from the putting stroke, and this grip establishes the basis for a firm, wristed stroke.

2

3

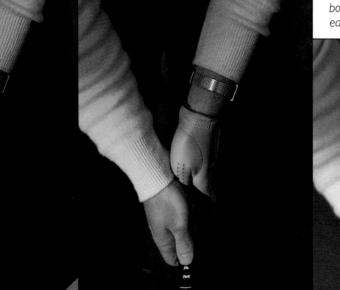

The completed grip shows both hands parallel to each other △3.

The palm of the right hand squarely faces the target △1.

With the fingers closed, the angle of the palm remains unchanged △2.

putting grip is to align the hands to the putter's face.

The putter should be gripped firmly, but never tightly. Many great putters concede that they grip the club very lightly. If you grip the club too firmly, the muscles in the forearms tense, and it is very hard to transmit any sort of feel from the putter face back up into the body to the brain. Also, because you are trying to make a smooth stroke it is easier if the muscles are relaxed.

Putting demands a very delicate stroke and so requires the greatest sensitivity in the hands and fingers. If you grip the club tightly it will inhibit this sensitivity. Good feel allows the golfer to respond to different textures of green or general putting conditions – putting in the rain, putting in the wind, putting down or up hill or putting on different grasses, for example.

THE CROSS-HANDED GRIP

A recent phenomenon in putting technique has been the emergence, in the last 10 years, of the cross-handed putting stroke. This method was originally used at the highest level by Bruce Lietzke, but it has been popularized on both sides of the Atlantic by Bernhard Langer, and now many top tournament players use it.

Because I am sure that the left hand controls the putting stroke, I believe that most of the players who now use the upside-down grip do so to eliminate the dominance of the right hand from the stroke. When the right hand is allowed to control the stroke, it can sometimes jerk the putter forward and make the ball go off line and too far. This is what the cross-handed putters are trying to avoid. When you grip the putter with the cross-handed technique, the right hand goes on the putter first. The club is held in the fingers, with the right thumb pointing straight down the shaft. The left hand is placed underneath the right, again with the thumbs down the top of the shaft and the club held in the fingers. From this position the right hand can stabilize the club, but the left hand is dominant and controls the amount of swing and speed judged necessary for the putt. The pull-through created with this cross-handed grip is exactly the same movement that you have tried to acquire when playing your long shots.

As with the conventional grip, the hands can be overlapped, interlocked or reverse overlocked, depending on which grip feels most comfortable. Most of the players who use the cross-handed grip seem to prefer the reverse overlap – that is, lapping the forefinger of the right hand over the little finger of the left in order to keep all four fingers of the left hand on the shaft and therefore in control. Because the left arm dominates the stroke, it pulls the putter through the ball, so that at impact, the top of the putter is slightly ahead of the bottom of the blade causing the ball to be struck around about its "equator" or just slightly above. This is fine as long as the putter is traveling horizontal to the ground and not in an arc down on to the

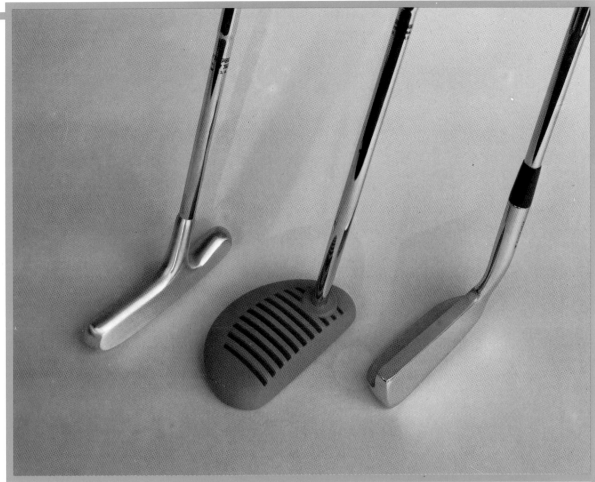

ball, and because the left hand is in control, there is nothing to stop you following through freely.

The stroking action is very similar to that of the putter who uses the ordinary hand and arm stroke with the grip the right way up. As with the conventional putting grips and putting stances, the eyes must be directly over the ball when you are using the cross-handed grip. The only slight difference will be in the stance, because the left hand is below the right with the cross-handed stroke, and the left shoulder will tend to be lower than it would be with the conventional stroke and the shoulders will be more level at the address. When making the stroke, the left hand and arm swing back together, and the angle between the back of the left hand and the back of the left arm should not vary throughout the stroke: it is very much an arm stroke.

THE STANCE

Once you have found the putter grip that is best for you, the next step is to find a comfortable stance. When you are adopting the stance to putt, there is one overriding requirement – your eyes must be directly above the ball at all times during the putting stroke. If your eyes are placed anywhere other than directly above the ball, your perspective of where you are hitting the ball will be distorted. If your eyes are inside the line of the putt, you will be inclined to hit the ball to the right of your target. If your eyes are outside the line of the putt, it is very easy to hit the ball left of

Three basic styles of putter are, left, the center-shaft, middle, the mallet and, right, the blade. There are many different types of putter, but all fall into these three basic categories.

the target.

Because your eyes are directly above the ball, the top of your spine will be horizontal with the ground. This means it is necessary to bend over to the ball and because most putters are only 33-36 inches long this is not difficult.

The next requirement is that you balance yourself properly. As with the longer shots, it is necessary to place your weight toward the balls of your feet, not locked back on your heels. By placing your weight in this position you are supporting your body weight with the muscles in your calves and your thighs, and you will find that you feel a slight degree of tension in these sets of muscles. Your arms need to be far enough from your body to allow you a free swing while you keep the rest of your body still.

You should adopt a square stance – that is, your feet should be the same distance from the target line. This will help you align the putter and maintain a virtual straight-back, straight-through stroke. If you adopt an open stance – that is, with your foot line aimed to the left of the line you want to swing the club along – or if you stand with your feet closed – that is, with your toe line pointing to the right of the line that you want to swing the club along – it will be more difficult for you to find the right line to swing the club along. If your feet are both the same distance from that line, the whole stance will be more symmetrical. It is not necessary for your feet to be a long way apart, although a wider stance does help to keep the body still during the putting stroke. Very few top golfers stand with their feet more than 12-15 inches apart, and some great putters – Ray Floyd in particular – stand with their feet very close together. The most important aspect of the stance is that you are balanced in such a way that your body does not move when you stroke the ball.

THE PUTTING STROKE

There is no need to swing quickly at the ball because you are not trying to hit the ball vast distances. The putting stroke should have a smooth, calm tempo, which should remain constant whether you are putting from a long or short distance. Once you have established your tempo for the short putt, the longer putt will have the same tempo, merely a longer stroke.

The second vital aspect of putting is a solid contact with the ball. To attain this you have to take two things into consideration. First, the putter face must be pointing in the direction that the ball should be traveling and, secondly, the putter must be accelerating when it comes into contact with the ball. You have to master these two skills before you can develop a "feel" for putting the ball a given distance. This "feel," or putting touch, as it is known, is the unconscious ability to hit the ball at exactly the right speed for the distance required. Anyone who hits the ball off center will miss the center by more on some putts than on others.

Top players use two distinct types of putting stroke. There is the long sweeping stroke, which is favored by most of the modern professionals. It has very little wrist action, and the putting stroke is made basically with the arms and shoulders. Then there is the jab stroke, which is a short wristy movement in which the arms and shoulders are kept still and only the wrists hinge.

The arm stroke tends to keep the putter lower to the ground and eliminates the possibility of hitting down or across the ball. This is considered a pressure-proof way of putting, a way that limits face rotation and keeps the club face pointing toward the target all the way through the stroke. Because the putter is swung just with the arms, it moves through a wider arc and the tempo of the stroke is considerably slower than the sharper jab stroke that is used by wrist putters.

The wrist putters hit the ball harder on the short putts, thereby eliminating some of the break that may be on the putt. They tend to putt the ball firmly into the back of the hole, whereas the arm putters tend to let it run in there softly. The greatest wrist putter of all time was Arnold Palmer, who holed more 6 foot-long second putts hard into the back of the hole than any other golfer. Over the years top players have used both methods, and neither has an edge over the other. Try both of them and find out which suits you and your temperament best. The great putters of today, such as Azinger, Faldo and Crenshaw, use

Top row At address the first essential is to build a stance that keeps the eyes directly over the ball. This is vital if the putt is to be aimed along the intended line ▷.

The putting stroke has to keep the blade of the club close to the ground, and this can be achieved only by using an arm and shoulder stroke. This type of stroke has the additional advantage that it keeps the face of the putter square to the target line ▷.

As the putter strikes the ball it will be following the path along which it was taken back. The body must be kept still while the stroke is being made. The pace of the putting stroke should be rhythmic and measured; therefore, the longer the putt, the longer the stroke ▷.

Bottom row A square stance helps to establish the correct line to the stroke. The ball should be positioned slightly forward in the stance and toward the left foot △. The putter's head is kept low to the ground by swinging

the arms and shoulders backwards and forward in a pendulum movement. Stroking the ball in this manner uses the big muscles of the body, which are less prone than the smaller ones to speed up and jerk △.

At impact, the face of the putter is traveling along the intended line of the putt. The head and body have remained still and should remain so until the end of the stroke △.

Bottom row *Once the ball has been hit, the putter follows through at least as far as it was taken back to make sure that the club is accelerating at impact. This is important when a solid strike on the ball is required. The follow-through guarantees a smooth roll on the ball, which is necessary when the distance of a putt has to be judged* ▷ *and* ▷.

Top row Putting practice is important to help acquire a judgment of distance. Successful putting is a combination of two elements – distance and direction – and of the two, judgment of distance is the harder to achieve. Constant practice will develop the ability to hit the ball at the right speed for the distance required. It is no coincidence that top players spend over half their practice time on the putting green.

The body has stayed in position and the putter has swung freely along the line of the putt △ . The temptation to look up and see where the ball has gone has been resisted △ .

5

a sweeping arm swing, which seems to make the ball roll at the same pace the whole length of the putt, while the old wrist putters used to make the ball start quickly and slow up quickly. The arm and shoulder putters have a follow-through about the same length as the backswing, whereas the jab, or tap, putters have virtually no follow-through. They liken the putting stroke to the action you would use if you had a drawing pin stuck in the back of the ball and you wanted to tap it further in with the putter.

You will keep the clubhead accelerating into the ball if you make sure that when you putt you keep your left hand in front of the putter's face and pull the clubhead through the ball. In this way, the putter's head will always be trying to catch up with the hands and strike the ball solidly. One tip that may help you to keep your putting stroke smooth is to remember that, before you take the club back, you should create a little forward press with your hands and move your hands very slightly toward the target. Then, when you move them back, bring the clubface back with a little rebound from your forward press position. This forward press is an independent movement with your hands and arms, and it should be done at the same pace that you want to create for your backswing tempo. When you push your hands forward make sure that you do not allow the face of the putter to open – that is, to point to the right of the target. When the hands are pushed forward in this manner the blade of the putter is able to start the reverse movement first, making it easier to keep your hands in front of the club throughout the stroke.

When they are lining up the putt, some pros, such as John Mahaffey, like to begin their routine by placing the putter's face in front of the golf ball and then moving it back

behind after they have squared it up to the target line. They feel that they can see the squareness of the blade better without the ball in the way. This practice of bringing the putter back behind the ball leaves the re-alignment open to error. Having the blade square in front of the ball does not mean that when you have moved it back an inch or two it will be square. However, I suggest you do some experimenting to determine how well this unique pre-swing key works for you.

STRIKING THE BALL

Several years ago, if you were faced with a downhill putt, which you did not want to hit past the hole, it was thought that you could ensure success by striking the ball nearer the toe of the putter because, when contact was made, its blade was raised slightly and some of the force would be lost from the shot. However, the problem is that when you hit the ball with the toe of the putter, its blade tends to open, so that the line along which you are trying to hit the ball is lost. Similarly, it used to be thought that if you have a putt that broke from right to left you should strike the ball in the toe of the putter so that you started the ball a little bit further right than you perhaps wanted to. These safety measures just aren't required if you read the putt properly and you know which line to hit it along. The same is true of striking the ball in the heel if the putt broke from left to right. There is no substitute for striking the ball solidly with the center of the putter.

When the ball is struck from the center of the putter, its blade does not deviate at all on contact with the ball, and the putt starts off in the direction in which the blade was aiming. When the ball is struck with the center of the putter, you have a better idea of the transfer of force from the putter to the ball and can therefore build up your putting touch, that subconscious ability to hit the ball at the desired speed. If you do not strike the ball in the sweet spot of the putter's face, you won't always strike it exactly the same distance away from the middle, and the amount of force you impart will vary with every stroke and make it impossible for you to judge distance accurately.

These days, the professionals putt so well that they feel they can hole anything, and it is not unusual for a top tournament player to have anything between 24 and 28 putts a round. This happens, of course, when they have missed the green and have chipped up so that their first putt is considerably closer than it would have been had they been on the green in regulation figures. There is no real distinction between a long and a short putt. The only time you notice it among the best players is when occasionally a couple of cross-handed putters will, from 10 feet or so away, revert to a normal grip. However, for the most part all the top professionals are trying to hole every first putt they can.

READING THE GREENS

Developing a mechanically perfect putting stroke will be of little use to you unless you can read greens – that is, learn to see the line on which the ball should be rolled into the hole and at what pace it should be struck in order to maintain that line. All putting greens have contours, and although they may look flat from a distance, there will always be some very slight undulation somewhere within the area of the green. When a ball is rolled across a slope, the law of gravity ensures that it will always roll in the same direction as the slope: the greater the slope, the more the ball will travel away from a straight line.

Therefore, the first consideration when approaching any green is to decide whether that part of the green between your ball and the hole is flat or whether there is one slope, or even more, on the line. A good way of deciding this is to stand behind your ball and imagine that you are striking your ball straight toward the hole. Look along the line and decide if the ball would roll away from that straight line and, if so, where. Should you decide that by striking the ball straight toward the hole it would finish 6 inches to the right of the hole, you would automatically decide to strike your putt 6 inches to the left of the hole. This is a positive way to read the green because you start off by looking at a straight line between your ball and the hole rather than standing behind your ball and trying to establish any line.

If you are putting across a consistent slope, the ball will break more as it slows down nearer to the hole than it will when it has just come off the putter. That is why it is particularly important to examine a 1 yard area around the hole before you putt. If there is any slope within this area, it will make your ball roll sideways more because in this area the ball will be rolling most slowly. It follows that when you are putting on fast greens you have to play for a maximum amount of break whereas when you are playing on slow or wet greens, the momentum will keep the ball traveling in a straighter line. Moreover, when you are putting on fast greens you tend to play the ball more slowly because by the time the ball reaches the hole any force on it will take it a considerable distance past. The same applies on dry greens or if you are putting with the wind behind you. The opposite applies on wet greens: then, you can afford to hit the ball a little straighter and a little harder without fear of it going too far past.

No green is perfectly flat, and the ability to judge accurately the amount the ground slopes and the distance the ball will deviate from a straight line is essential to successful putting.

UPHILL AND DOWNHILL PUTTS

You should also take into consideration whether you are putting up- or downhill. Remember, when you are putting uphill the ball can go into the hole a little bit more quickly because the back of the hole will be higher than the front; on downhill putts it pays to be a little more cautious and to try and let the putt die into the hole.

SIDE-HILL PUTTS

When faced with a side-hill putt, most amateurs tend to miss the ball on the low side of the cup, and the low side of the cup has, in fact, become known as the "amateur side" while the high side is known as the "pro side." This has happened over the years because the professionals tend to strike their putts more firmly and get the ball past the hole more often than amateurs.

More putts are missed through indecision than all the other causes put together. Indecision begins with an inability to decide whether the ball will roll straight or whether it will curve when it is rolled into the hole. The professionals are not afraid of allowing for break, and they play freely and firmly forward. Amateurs, on the other hand, tend to decide there may be some break, but they are not really sure so they try to hit the ball straight at the hole: because of the indecision caused by the inability to read the green, they never hit the ball hard enough, and their indecision shows up in their putting stroke.

The importance of reading the green cannot be over-emphasized. Some great players like Lee Trevino stalk their putts from all sides, walking completely around their ball and around the hole. Other professionals prefer to read their putt from two places, directly behind the ball and directly behind the hole. They look at the putt from behind the hole as well as from behind the ball to confirm their ability to read the green. When walking from behind the ball to behind the hole they will usually walk on what they believe is the low side of the putt, because the slope is more visible from below than it is from above. As they look at the line of the putt from behind the hole they are merely confirming what they read from behind the ball.

I am not a great believer in the "never up, never in" school of thought of putting. If you miss a putt, you want it to stay as close as possible to the edge of the hole to make your next putt as easy as possible. The idea of hitting the ball so hard that it will go past the hole can distort your natural feel for the putt. An advantage of putting the ball past the hole is that it shows the line for the one back. When you are faced with your second putt you do know the direction in which the green slopes, and that is the only reason to want to knock your first putt past the hole.

The time to begin your mental preparation for reading the green is as soon as your ball finishes on the putting surface. Look at the general contour of the green as you walk toward it, because this can help you judge the direction of the break when you come to line up your putt.

ASSESSING THE BREAK

The best way to read the line of a putt is to bring the eye as close to the ground as possible. This should be done about 10 feet directly behind the ball. If a clear picture cannot be obtained from this position, then it is a good idea to check the line from behind the hole.

In addition to reading the slopes on the greens, it is necessary to judge the pace of the greens. On a fast green the ball is struck less firmly and the slope has more effect on the line of the putt. It is quite possible on a putt of 30 feet on a fast green to have to allow for a break of 5 feet, whereas the same putt on a slow green may only break by about 1 foot. On long putts the break is less effective on the early part of the putt when the ball is traveling at its fastest, but as the ball slows down by the hole the break will take maximum effect. Besides looking for slopes across the line of a putt, it is important to check whether the putt is up or downhill. Often the best way to ascertain the overall slope of a green is from a distance, and this can be done when approaching the green from the fairway. During practice rounds, good players are looking to put their approach shots in a position below the hole so that they leave themselves uphill putts from where it is easier to attack the hole.

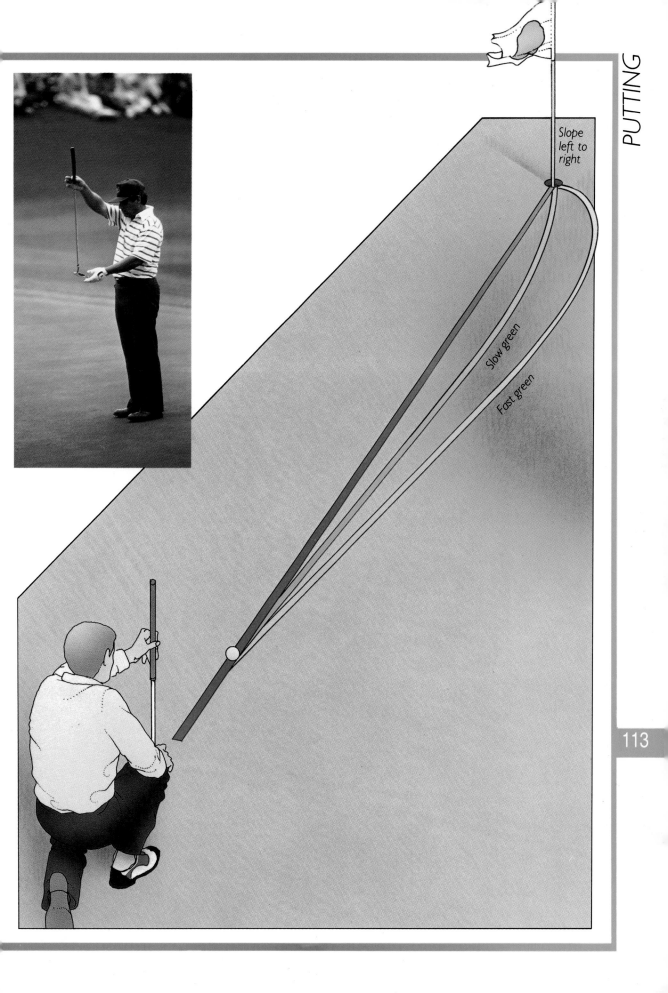

Slope
left to
right

Slow green

Fast green

Lee Trevino goes to more
trouble stalking a putt
than perhaps any other
player. After looking along
the line of a putt from
behind the ball, Trevino
walks in a circle right
around the back of the
hole and back to his ball
without taking his eyes off
the line of his putt. This
routine settles his mind on
the line of the putt and
enables him to execute
the putting stroke without
further deliberation.

6

SPECIALIST SHOTS

I f golf were played over totally flat terrain, it would be a very dull game indeed. The fact that golf courses are laid out on rolling terrain, which threads its way between trees, bushes and streams, means that the golfer faces a variety of different lies and is often forced to shape a shot around an obstacle. In this chapter we will look at how the ball will react from certain lies, how the ball can be shaped in different directions and trajectories, and how the weather can affect the performance of both the player and shots to be played.

TARGET

To use the imagination when playing shots from unusual lies. To establish certain principles which apply when the length and trajectory of a shot are compromised by the conditions.

ACHIEVEMENT

A realization that no matter how hopeless the situation, an imaginative approach can help conjure up an excellent recovery shot.

Bernhard Langer

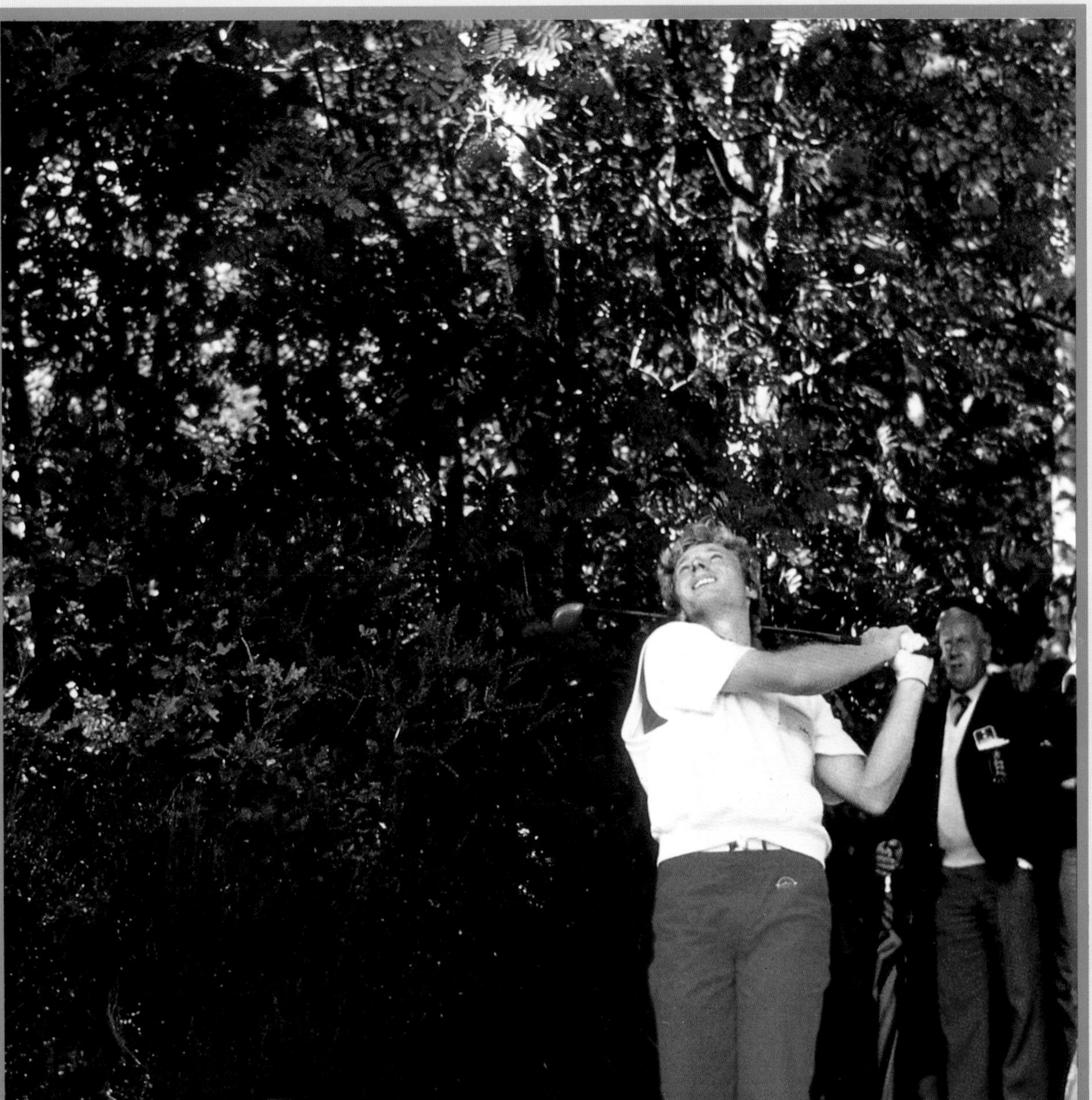

Imagination can sometimes rescue seemingly impossible situations. Greg Norman shows that by reversing the club and playing the shot left-handed he can extract the ball from under some low tree branches and save himself a penalty stroke. The important point to remember with this kind of shot is not to be too ambitious and just make sure the ball is hit clear of the trouble to make the next shot easier.

THE DRAW AND FADE

The two most commonly shaped shots – that is, shots that are deliberately bent in one direction or the other by the golfer – are known as the draw and the fade. The draw is a shot that starts slightly to the right of target and that bends to the left. The fade is the opposite: it starts slightly to the left of the target and bends to the right.

SHAPING SHOTS

The ability to bend the ball is a skill that has been developed by all the great players. The main reasons for acquiring this skill are to maneuvre the ball around obstacles and to negate the effect of cross-winds. A shot that bends from right to left is known as a draw; a shot that bends from left to right is a fade. Most good players base their game on one or the other of these two shot patterns.

Ball flight left to right

Target line

Ball flight right to left

Fade

Draw

THE DRAW

To develop the draw, set up as if you were playing a straight shot but aim to the right of your target leaving the clubface aimed straight at the target. If you swing normally along the line that you have set up – that is, to the right of the target – the clubface will be closed to this line at impact, and a hook spin will be applied to the ball, making it curve from right to left in the air. The trajectory of the ball will be lower than normal, and the ball will travel farther. Most of this extra distance will be roll after the ball has landed; so when you play a drawn or hooked shot, it is important to remember to use less club than you normally require for a straight shot.

It is not necessary to change the basic swing to draw the ball from right to left. The only adjustments required are that the player aims the body and swings to the right of the target while aiming the clubface directly toward the target. Aiming to the right in this manner effectively moves the ball toward the right foot in the stance ⚠ and ▷.

Top row *Viewed from behind, it is clear that the clubhead swings further inside the target line than it would do from a square stance △₂. At the top of the backswing the club is deeper – that is, more behind the player – than it would be when a straight* shot is played △₃. *Because the club is approaching the ball from further inside the target line, the arms and hands have to rotate more to square up the clubface △₄. It is this rotation that applies the anti-clockwise spin to the ball △₅.*

2

Bottom row *Because the club is moving further inside the target line, the shoulders are pulled further around in the backswing and a stronger, deeper position is achieved at the top ▷₂ and ▷₃.*

From halfway down, extra hand and arm rotation is necessary to square up the face at impact. The head and upper body must be kept behind the ball ▷₄ and ▷₅.

Through the ball, the hands and arms have rotated sufficiently to impart right-to-left spin on the ball 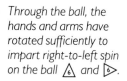 and ▷.

The extra rotation of the hands and arms pulls the club into a flatter plane at the finish of the swing. This is shown by the position of the hands at the end of the follow-through: they will be around the left shoulder rather than above it △ and ▷.

124

6

6

7

7

THE FADE

To fade the ball aim to the left of the target along the line on which you wish to start the shot and open the clubface to aim it at the target. The club is still swung in the normal way along the line of the set up – that is, left of target – but the open clubface will produce a slicing blow at impact that will make the ball curve left to right in flight. The effective loft of the club is increased because the clubface is open to the line of swing, making sliced shots rise higher and travel shorter distances. Remember, therefore, that when trying to fade the ball, use more club.

Two of the most successful players in the history of the game, Ben Hogan and Lee Trevino, adopted the fade as their standard shot pattern. This type of shot is a combination of left-to-right spin and backspin, which exhausts the ball's energy during its upward climb. The ball then drops softly on the ground, eliminating the unpredictable roll that is a product of the draw.

To prepare for the fade shot, the body is aimed to the left of the target following the line along which the ball is required to start. The clubface is pointed toward the target. Opening the stance in this fashion has the effect of moving the ball toward the left foot △ and ▷.

Top row At the start of the backswing the club is swung back along the line of the feet, ▷ which takes it outside the target line ▷. Because the body is aimed to the left, it is not possible to turn the shoulders behind the ball, and this creates mainly an arm swing. At impact, the hips are turned further to the left than normal, and this pulls the left hand slightly further ahead of the ball ▷. This helps to prevent the clubface from turning over during the follow-through. ▷.

2

126

Bottom row Because the open body position restricts the turn of the shoulders, the arms lift the club to the top of the backswing △ and △. The movement of the body in the downswing as it unwinds further to the left enables the hands to be ahead of the ball and to keep the face open at impact △. In the follow-through, the left arm stays straight longer and the right hand does not climb over the left △.

LOW AND HIGH SHOTS

Low shots require some slight alterations in the address position. First, play the ball further back in the center of the stance, which should be a little wider than normal; second, hold the club toward the bottom of the grip; and third, place more weight on the left leg. Your hands should be well in front of the ball at address. The wider stance and the weight on the left side will help to keep the backswing shorter than normal, and the ball should be hit with a punching action, which curtails the follow-through. When you are hitting a low shot, take more club than you need, because you do not want the ball to spin too much as this will make it climb and defeat your objective.

To hit the ball high also requires several changes in the address position. Take up a slightly narrower stance, with the ball position just inside the left heel, and hold the club at the very top of the grip. These changes make it easier to achieve a long backswing and an even longer follow-through. Make sure that the head is kept well behind the shot all the way through the swing, and remember that an open clubface will help you to get the ball up quickly.

In playing both low and high shots it is important to remember that the length of swing is the dominating factor in the trajectory of the ball. The short punch swing makes the ball fly low because the acceleration of the clubhead occurs only over a short distance; therefore, all the energy is exploded into the back of the ball. The long swing has a more even tempo, and the acceleration is spread over a greater arc; therefore, because the clubface is not accelerating as quickly, the club is allowed to run under the ball more and the high follow-through helps to keep the arc shallow and lift it high into the air.

OVERCOMING OBSTACLES

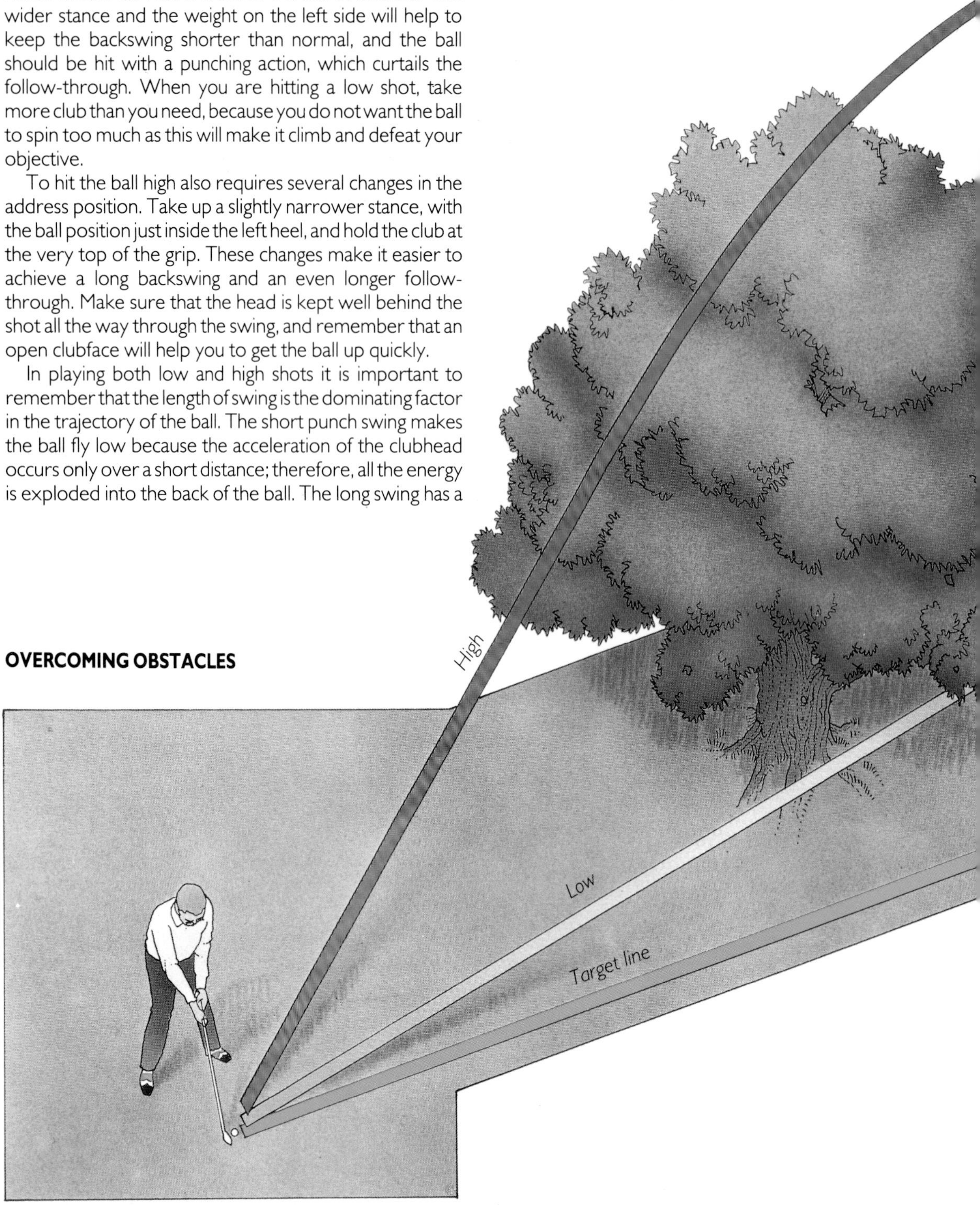

High

Low

Target line

Left *Many professionals claim it is more necessary to have the skill deliberately to hit the ball high or low than it is to be able to draw or fade the ball. The high shot is useful*

Top right *At address for the low shot, the ball should be played further back in the stance, the weight should favor the left foot, and the hands should hold the club at the bottom of the grip (inset) and be kept ahead of the blade of the club.*

Bottom right *At address for the high shot, the ball should be played further forward in the stance, with*

when you have to play over banks or trees; the low shot is vital if you want to keep the ball under the wind or under low-hanging tree branches. Another reason for hitting the ball high is to stop it quickly on the greens, whereas on fast-running, hard courses the low running shot is sometimes the only one that can be played.

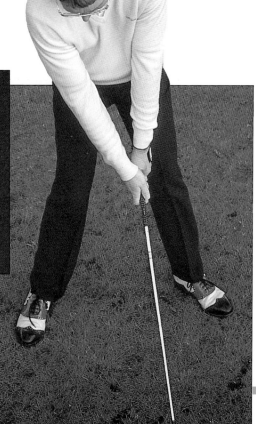

the weight favoring the right foot. The club should be held at the very top of the grip (inset) and the hands are directly behind the clubface at address.

UNUSUAL LIES

The more interesting golf courses are built on rolling terrain, which means that your ball very rarely finishes on a completely flat piece of ground. There are four ways in which the slope of the ground can make your shot more difficult: the ball can be below your feet or above your feet, and you can either be playing downhill or uphill. You may also have to face a combination of any two of these four conditions.

BALL BELOW FEET

Each shot requires its own technique if you are to control where you want the ball to go. We will start with the ball that is lying below your feet. Because the ball is lower than your feet, the angle of the plane of your swing is steeper. Therefore, you have to stand, without thinking about it, closer to the ball. You must not make any conscious effort to change your stance, but the fact that the ball is lower than your feet will automatically draw you closer to it. Once you have done that, play the ball with as near your normal swing as you can possibly produce. It is impossible for golfers to develop separate swings for all the separate lies that face them on a golf course. You only have the one swing, and this must be adapted to every shot you play.

BALL ABOVE FEET

When the ball is lying higher than your feet, the converse occurs because the ball is closer to the center of your swing arc. Therefore, when you establish your natural swing radius, you will automatically stand further from the ball. This is not a conscious decision: you will adopt the position naturally, purely by defining your normal radius with your left arm and the club shaft. Again, keep your technique as near to normal as possible, because the lie of the land will force changes upon you that you will cope with perfectly well with your normal method. It is only if you allow yourself to get mentally disturbed at the thought of the ball being above or below your feet that panic sets in and the shot becomes really difficult.

It is worth noting that when the ball is above your feet it tends to hook in flight off a good swing, and when it is below your feet it will tend to slice in flight off a good swing. Therefore, when you aim yourself in these lies, you should make allowance for this movement of the ball through the air. On extreme slopes keep as still as you can and play the shot with your arms and hands only, hitting it forward half the distance you would normally make with the club and making sure you contact the ball and move it to a better, flatter spot in the fairway. This is a far better course of action than going for broke with an unbalanced swing from an uneven lie, when there is every likelihood that you will produce a disastrous shot.

UPHILL LIE

The other two lies are less usual but still have to be coped with during the round: they are the downhill and the uphill lie. When you are playing uphill, you should try to get your set up as near to normal as possible. The fact that your left foot is higher than your right will automatically throw your weight back on to your right leg. It is important to try to remain at right angles to the ground, so you will be tilted back a bit more than you would be on level ground. When you hit the ball, your weight tends to hang back behind and the clubface will close a little, and the tendency is to pull the shot straight to the left. This should be allowed for when you aim yourself to play this type of shot.

DOWNHILL LIE

When playing a downhill shot the opposite occurs and your body will tend to be tilted forward in front of the

Below left *Because the ball is below the feet, the player has to stand closer to it in order to reach it. The player must bend more from the waist and allow the arms to position themselves closer to the body. Because the ball is closer to the feet, the plane of the swing is forced to be more upright.*

shot with your weight on the left side. This stance can produce a shot that is pushed straight to the right; so when you set yourself up you must allow for this.

When you are playing uphill or downhill shots it is essential that you keep your body at right angles to the ground. Lean with the ground, and do not play with your higher leg bent and your lower leg straight. You must try to create as near a normal address position as you can. If you have one sound technique you will be able to adapt it for all the lies that you get on the golf course, but if you try to develop a fresh swing for every different lie, you will find the game will become far too complicated.

I see more people struggle with uneven lies because

they have persuaded themselves that they need to create a different swing to cope with the conditions of the lie. They miss more shots because of this than for any other reason. I cannot emphasize too strongly that if you have a good technique a small thing like an uneven lie will not undermine your ability to hit the ball.

Below center *The important thing about playing an uphill shot is to try and keep the body at right angles to the slope. The uphill lie creates a feeling of falling back with all the weight on the right side. This makes the weight transference on the downswing difficult and usually leads to a pulled shot.*

Below right *The address position for the downhill lie automatically places most of the body weight on to the left leg. This restricts body turn in the backswing, and the player tends to move ahead of the ball at impact. This can create pushed shots to the right, so allowances should be made when aiming this shot.*

PLAYING FROM A DIVOT

One of the most frustrating circumstances in golf is to hit a perfect tee shot only to find that it has finished in a divot hole in the middle of a fairway. This "rub of the green" can be extremely irritating, but, if you use a little common sense, it need not cost you any shots. If the ball is in the back of the divot hole, it is not such a serious problem. Make your normal swing, trying not to hit at the ball, and make sure you follow-through. The worst thing that could happen is that you may catch the ball thin – that is, not quite at the bottom – and it will fly lower and roll further than you anticipated. Even so, it should finish in your target area. If you try to dig the ball out by chopping down on it, you considerably increase the possibility of error, and your worst shot will be a "fat" one, which will go no distance at all. The shot from the middle of the divot is played as nearly as possible to a normal shot, but with the emphasis once again on the follow through. This helps to make the ball fly and eliminates the chop from the swing, which would be disastrous in this situation.

The first thing to do when the ball is in the front of the divot is to recognize that it will limit your ability to achieve distance. Once you decide how far you can hit the shot, take the most lofted club that will produce that distance, then swing down and through the ball making sure that your hands are ahead of the blade at impact.

Below When the ball lies in a divot hole, the address position is exactly the same as it would be for a normal shot. No compensations are required, because a normal swing provides the best chance for a successful recovery.

132

PLAYING OUT OF ROUGH

If your ball lies in heavy rough you may have a problem when the long grass wraps itself around the shaft of the club on both the back- and downswings, making it difficult to control the alignment of the clubface. The best way to deal with this is to address the ball with the club above the grass and the face slightly open. Then lift the club as straight upwards as you can and drop it down slightly behind the ball as you would if you were playing a sand shot. Do not try to follow through. Let the sole of the club slide under the ball and pop it straight up into the air

⚠ *When playing from heavy rough, the ball should be positioned back toward the right foot in the stance because this is the one occasion in golf when a wide, shallow swing will not be effective.*

⚠ *The club is lifted straight up in the air on the backswing. There is no shoulder or hip turn, and the weight is kept equally balanced on both feet. The feeling of the backswing is definitely a "lift" of the club and not a swing.*

through the grass. The steep angle of descent will reduce the amount of grass that can wrap itself around the shaft and prevent the face from closing too much. Grass tends to wrap itself around the hosel and shaft of the club which slows it down, but it does not slow down the toe of the club, which keeps going quickly and turns over into a closed position. When you are playing out of rough there is always a chance that the ball will fly to the left of where you aimed. It will also fly lower with a closed clubface and have more roll on it than a normal shot; so remember to allow for this when you are setting up the shot. You should also remember that the grass in the rough will come between the clubface and the ball when you strike the ball, and in so doing eliminate the chance of any backspin. This is another reason why the ball will fly lower and roll more when it lands.

ARNOLD PALMER

Arnold Palmer, whose tremendous physical strength makes light of heavy rough, pitches from deep rough. Note how the rough has stopped the club from following through, although Palmer has been able to force the club through on to the ball.

5

⚠3 and ⚠4 *The downswing is just a steep chop with the arms aimed at striking rough 1 inch behind the ball. If any attempt were made to sweep the ball out of long rough, the grass would wrap itself around the shaft of the club, slowing it down and turning the clubface over.*

⚠5 *No attempt should be made to follow through because the direction of the stroke has been so steeply downward.*

4

BAD WEATHER PLAY

Extreme weather conditions can turn an enjoyable round of golf into a frustrating nightmare, but few players allow this to prevent them playing, and the best players accept bad weather as an extra challenge.

Only two types of weather condition prevent golf from being played. One is so much rain or snow that the course is covered and the holes filled with water. Within the Rules of Golf rain and snow are defined as "casual water." The other condition is the lightning that accompanies thunderstorms at the end of very hot spells. Never play when there is lightning around. If you get caught out on the course, stop playing and get away from the open spaces, find a hollow to lie down in or make for the safety of the nearest shelter. Even the biggest tournaments are postponed and play is held up during electric storms. Leave your clubs where they are, and go back and get them later. Don't carry them them with you because the steel shafts make wonderful lightning conductors. Never take shelter under a single big tree, for that again will attract the lightning. Many people are killed on golf courses each year because they make the mistake of trying to hide under trees rather than find proper shelter.

WET WEATHER

It is very difficult to play good golf in heavy rain. The wet grass makes it more difficult to control the ball because moisture gets between the ball and the clubhead and reduces the amount of the spin that should be put on the ball. When the ground is very wet it is not unusual to see players consistently hit the ball 20 or 30 yards further than they want, purely because of this phenomenon. These shots, which are called flyers, are totally impossible to judge. The most recent development in golf club design – square grooves cut into the faces of iron clubs – was developed specifically to eliminate this one shot. When the ball strikes the face of a club with square grooves in it, the water is squashed down into the groove and the face is able to make contact with the ball. Using a club with square grooves really does eliminate flyers, especially from the rough, because not only is the water forced into the grooves but some of the grass that would normally be trapped between the clubface and the ball is held there too, allowing the golfer to get much more solid contact with the ball.

Rain can be extremely disturbing, especially if you wear glasses. When it gets in your eyes or on your glasses it tends to make it very difficult to judge distances. One solution is to wear a cap with a big peak, or to wear a sun visor. Then at least the water will only impair your distance judgments because you will be unable to see your target clearly. Keep a dry towel in your golf bag, and when it starts to rain tie it into the spokes of your umbrella. Your towel should keep dry under the umbrella and allow you to dry your hands. Remember that your clubs will get wet just lying in your bag as rain runs down the shafts and on to the grips; so make sure you dry the grips too. In wet weather one of the great advantages of having a caddie is that he can take care of the clubs for you, and all you have to worry about is keeping your hands dry. Although an umbrella is vital in wet weather, if there is a strong wind as well it becomes something of an encumbrance.

As far as playing conditions are concerned, you must remember that when it is wet on the greens you have to strike the ball a little bit harder with your putter and hit the ball harder for your shots from around the green because the ball won't run quite as far as it would on a dry day. Try to keep your chip shots in the air a little bit longer before allowing them to roll and when pitching the ball, remember that the ball will stop more quickly as the rain softens the surface of the greens.

In bunkers, wet sand gets packed down harder, and if you make a normal swing the ball will come out faster. You have to remember to take a slightly easier swing and put less force into it. If you are in a shallow trap, it may be easier actually to chip the ball – that is, don't take sand at all – just as you would if you were on a bare spot on the fairway the same distance from the hole.

WIND

Wind is the ultimate hazard for all golfers. It does not blow constantly, and apart from affecting the flight of the ball it also has a great effect on a player's balance as well. Even the greatest professionals have trouble playing in the wind. When you are trying to get into a stable position at address, it is usually a good idea to crouch just a little more, bending

Above A close-up showing square grooves. The water is able to run away through this type of groove, thereby allowing more of the clubface to make contact with the ball without any water interposing between.

your knees and trying to make a tighter contact with the ground. Because of the difficulty in balancing, it is probably a good idea never to hit full out when you are playing in a fierce wind. Always take more club than you think you need, and when you make your swing, execute the backswing without making a great turn of the hips. Keep the hips as still as you can, and your body, therefore, more centered over the ball. Pull through hard with your left arm. Because you have taken more club you don't have to swing as hard, and as a result you create less backspin. Backspin carries the ball up into the air, and this is not required in windy conditions. It is also difficult to control the club on little chips. The wind tends to blow the club away from the line you are trying to swing along, and, as you are not swinging it very quickly, the wind has plenty of time to affect the club. This aspect of wind play is the one that worries the professionals most of all.

It is very hard to putt when the club is being blown around in your hands, and to add to the problem the ball tends to oscillate on the green. Many professionals do not ground the club behind the ball in a strong wind, so that, because they have not addressed the ball, they cannot be penalized if it moves.

Although the main reason for playing with a wide stance is that it restricts the turn of the hips in the backswing, in windy conditions this wider stance will be invaluable because a sudden gust could unbalance you at the top of your backswing. The wider stance helps to keep you over the ball and more in control.

USING THE WIND

In spite of the physical problems, the most important thing about playing in the wind is to get into the right frame of mind. Too many golfers fight the wind instead of using it, and wind unsettles average players so much that they worry about what the wind will do to their shots, trying to hit them harder and only succeeding in hitting them worse. When you are playing an iron shot, the wind will make a difference of one or two clubs to the distance the ball will have to travel. You have to accept this fact and let the club produce the shot: don't try to beat it to death. Whether you are playing with or against the wind remember that if you lose 10 yards against the wind on one hole, you are going to gain that distance downwind on the next hole. When the wind is behind you, don't try to hit too hard off the tee: tee the ball up a little higher than normal or even use a 3 wood, but do not hit too hard. You should take plenty of swing, which will get the ball up into the air for you, and remember that the rhythm and tempo of your game should be very much at the forefront of your mind.

In a cross wind the ordinary player will be better off if he allows for some drift in his shot. Some professionals try to play it the opposite way. For example, if the wind is blowing from right to left, a professional who can control the ball will try to fade the shot left to right, aiming at the hole and letting the wind balance the drift of his shot. The average golfer, however, cannot afford to lose the distance that is given up when you play this type of shot; he will do better to aim off to the right by the amount he thinks the wind will move his ball and then allow it to. The ball will then travel the maximum distance. Remember, a following wind tends to minimize the effect of hooks and slices, while a wind against the shot exaggerates these faults.

It is impossible to predict what kind of bounce a ball flying with the wind will take. Any strength you put on it at impact will usually be exaggerated both while the ball is in the air and after it comes down. For example, when the ball slices with the wind it will bounce to the right when it hits the ground. When you are playing downwind, the biggest problem will be to stop the ball where you want, and usually you should pitch the ball many yards short of the target and allow it to roll up to it. A low shot is sometimes more effective than a high one when you are playing downwind because it bounces and rolls without the great acceleration that the wind provides.

Above *Wet weather need not be a handicap if the proper equipment is used. Modern waterproof rainsuits are designed to* *give the player room to swing while still looking smart. The hood over the bag will keep the clubs and grips dry.*

137

It must be emphasized that you do not need to change your basic technique when you are playing in the wind. If you are aiming into the wind, take plenty of club and hold your hands a little further forward than you might normally do at address. This keeps the clubface slightly closed and helps the ball to fly on a lower trajectory. Moreover, if you miss the ball from this position, it will tend to hook a little but still go forward and penetrate the wind. If the ball is hit into the wind with an open clubface, all you will get is a very soft, short, wide slice. As long as you take plenty of club to play into the wind, you don't need to swing any harder than you do normally – the extra distance is in the club – although the temptation to hit harder than you need is always there.

If you are playing in cold weather, make sure you are dressed warmly to keep your muscles soft and supple, but

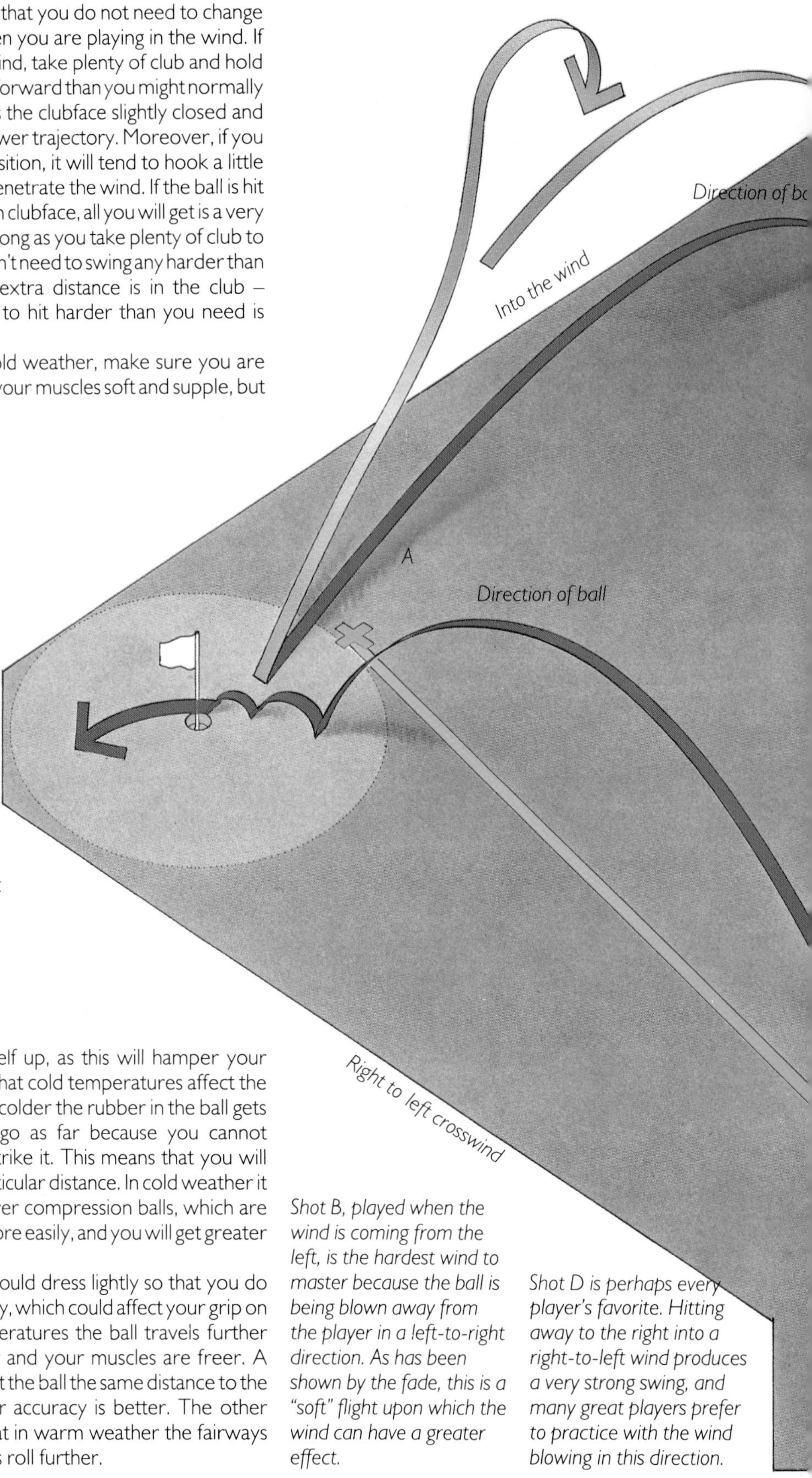

WIND PLAY

This simple but effective diagram shows how the wind can affect golf shots in four basic ways. Shot A, played directly into the wind, requires a longer club because the wind will reduce the distance the ball flies. It will also exaggerate the result of an off-center hit.

Shot C, downwind, requires a much shorter club because the extra loft of the club will maximize the height on the shot and enable the wind to help the ball. The ball will also roll further on landing.

try not to bundle yourself up, as this will hamper your swing. Remember, too, that cold temperatures affect the ball. As the weather gets colder the rubber in the ball gets harder, and it will not go as far because you cannot compress it when you strike it. This means that you will need more club for a particular distance. In cold weather it is a good idea to use lower compression balls, which are designed to compress more easily, and you will get greater distance.

In hot weather you should dress lightly so that you do not become hot and sticky, which could affect your grip on the club. In higher temperatures the ball travels further because the air is lighter and your muscles are freer. A shorter club which will get the ball the same distance to the green and improve your accuracy is better. The other thing to remember is that in warm weather the fairways are dry and the tee shots roll further.

Shot B, played when the wind is coming from the left, is the hardest wind to master because the ball is being blown away from the player in a left-to-right direction. As has been shown by the fade, this is a "soft" flight upon which the wind can have a greater effect.

Shot D is perhaps every player's favorite. Hitting away to the right into a right-to-left wind produces a very strong swing, and many great players prefer to practice with the wind blowing in this direction.

Direction of ball

Into the wind

A

Direction of ball

Right to left crosswind

Direction of ball

Left to right crosswind

B

Wind direction

Direction of ball

C

Downwind

D

7 PREPARING TO COMPETE

The challenge of golf is two-fold. First, there is the challenge of pitting your game against the golf course; second, there is the challenge of competing against other golfers. Both these challenges create psychological pressures, but these can be largely eliminated if you prepare carefully. Confidence breeds success, and confidence in your swing should be built on the practice ground. Practicing a variety of shots will equip you for similar situations that occur in actual play, and an honest appraisal of your own ability will help you to plan your way around the course.

▶ TARGET ◀

To ensure that the fullest preparations are made before making the opening shot and how correct mental applications can bring success.

ACHIEVEMENT

Understanding the necessity of warming up and how accessories such as cards, yardage charts, markers and tees are essential to competing successfully.

Severiano Ballesteros loosening up on the practice tee before competing in the Open Championship.

All tournament professionals spend hours on the practice ground refining their method. Many of them work with a particular teacher such as Bernhard Langer seen here working with his coach Willie Hoffman. Close relationships like these mean that a coach will know a player's game so well that the slightest fault can be quickly spotted and put right immediately.

PRACTICE

Golf is unusual in that the best players are not the players who hit the best shots; they are the players who hit the best bad shots. The best players are those who, when they swing at the ball, have a very good idea of the way it is going to finish up. They may not hit the ball straight all the time, they may slice the ball with every shot they hit, but, as long as they know that the ball is going to fade, they can allow for it and be very competitive players. The trick is not to let your ego get in your way. It is no good fading nine shots out of ten into the fairway and hitting the tenth one straight, and spending your life aiming straight at the target. You must work with the percentages and allow for the fade that you know is going to be there.

In order to develop a consistent pattern to your game, it is vital that you learn to practice. The practice tee is a garage in which the car is built; the golf course is the racetrack on which it races. The first essential when you set out to practice is to have a target – that is, you must decide what you want from your practice session. You may decide that you want to improve your chipping or to stop slicing the ball as badly as you have done in the past. Whatever aspect of your game you select, work on that one thing for 30 to 35 minutes and then have a rest. It is far better to have four half-hour practice sessions than to have one two-hour practice session. This is because you won't be tired at the end of half-an-hour and will be anxious to continue. Also, if your practice has been bad for that half hour it will not have a damaging effect on your game. During a half-hour session tiredness will not become a problem.

Every practice shot should be aimed at an actual target, and the results of each shot should be checked to analyze

Right An exercise to stretch the muscles in the back. Stand erect and hold the club across the back of your shoulders △. Turn gently to the right △ and back to the left △. Repeat, turning slightly further each time, until you can turn 90 degrees in either direction.

what happened on each swing, good or bad. Golfers tend to assume good shots as of right, but they must be analyzed in just the same way as the bad ones.

There is an important distinction between practicing and warming up. The warm-up consists of hitting 20 or 30 balls before a round, and the idea is to loosen the muscles and to find out how your swing is behaving on that particular day and which way the ball is flying so that when you get on the first tee you have some idea of what to expect. This is totally different from a practice session, which is a period of time spent hitting golf balls and analyzing the reasons why a ball flew well or badly. On the practice ground the golfer is thinking about causes and accepts that the results might be of secondary importance.

Above An exercise to loosen the lower body. Place a club across the lower back and hook it into place with both elbows △. Stand erect and turn gently to the right △ and then back again to the left △. Repeat, turning slightly further each time until the lower back muscles become supple.

144

This is different from playing, where results are the only important thing.

CHECKPOINTS FOR PRACTICE

The first thing to check when you are practicing is your grip. This is the cornerstone on which your swing is built and it is very hard to make constructive adjustments to your swing if your grip is bad. It will stop you developing your swing along sound principles because it will distort the angles for which you should be striving. You can practice your grip at home or in the office, in fact, anywhere you can stand up and hold a golf club in front of you. Remember, when you practice your grip, that you must first place the club in the right position – that is, tilted, slightly forward, with the top of the shaft in front of the face.

It is hardly worth practicing any golf without actually hitting the ball. The best swings in the world are wasted on

Below A good exercise for loosening the arms. Assume the address position, holding the club with one hand at the top of the grip and the other on the clubhead △.

Swing the right arm back behind the neck ⚠ and swing the arms in the opposite direction until the left arm is behind the neck ⚠.

145

Right *A good loosening exercise is to swing three clubs at once. Start by just making short swings and gradually increase the length until you are making a full swing. Do not start with a full swing because the weight of three clubs could easily cause a muscle strain. An added bonus of this exercise is that the extra weight cannot be swung quickly, and so the warm up can be achieved with a slow, easy rhythm.*

dandelions. If practice is going to be progressive, you must be building feel and touch into your game, and there is no way you can add that to your memory bank if you are not actually striking a golf ball. There is no feel to a swing that doesn't have a ball in the way of it. In the old days, some professionals would not let their pupils hit a golf ball until they had six lessons. But golf is all about controlling golf balls, and the sooner you become familiar and comfortable with a golf club and a golf ball, and putting the two together, the sooner you will become a proficient golfer.

The only way to practice your stance is to stand in front of a mirror or to have a friend check the stance. Your weight should be toward the balls of the feet, with your body weight supported by the muscles in the calves and thighs. Your body should be leaning forward from the waist, while your arms hang clear of your chest so that they can swing freely. You should not be so close to the ball that you feel your ribs are in the way of your arm swing, nor so far away that you feel yourself stretching and tensing.

One of the most positive benefits of practice is a good routine for setting yourself up over the ball. It requires considerable patience to stand behind the ball, walk to the side of it, have a practice swing, put your club behind the ball with your feet together, place the right foot in position and then bring the left foot into position have your waggle and swing. Only by going through this routine time after time in your practice sessions will it become automatic.

Some modern tournament professionals place the club behind the ball and hold it with just their right hand. This method is not to be recommended because it tends to align the club shaft to the right arm rather than the left where it should be. It is better to grip the club before you walk to the ball. The less time you spend standing over the ball the better, and having to build your grip while you are standing there will only add to the confusion. A great advantage of placing your grip on the club before you approach the ball is that it makes you pick out a target to aim at, and this helps to increase confidence.

Right *If you have given yourself time to prepare properly before a round of golf, you should pay particular attention to the scoring shots. These are the little pitch and chip shots, which, if played correctly, will roll three shots into two. An excellent way of establishing a feel for these short shots, is to stick an open umbrella into the ground and to try to chip balls into it from varying distances.*

3

147

Even the best players need advice on their swings. Many of them find a regular teacher to whom they repair frequently to fine tune their games. Nick Faldo **(right)** the 1987 Open Champion, is advised by David Leadbetter. Tom Watson practices under the watchful eye of Byron Nelson **(below left)**; and Sam Torrance works with his lifelong teacher, his father Bob **(far right)**. Even under competitive circumstances, the professionals help each other out at tournaments, and here Gary Player discusses a point with Jack Nicklaus **(below right)**.

COMPETITIVE GOLF

There are four basic requirements for being competitive at golf. Bear them in mind and your game should improve immeasurably. They are:

● **A sound and simple swing technique;**

● **A good short game;**

● **An honest appraisal of your game;**

● **A good strategy.**

A SOUND AND SIMPLE SWING

Of all the requirements, a sound and simple swing is the most important because it can be repeated time after time, and that breeds confidence and consistency, the two most vital elements of winning. In the previous chapters we have seen how the most consistent swing is the one in which the club is pulled on to the ball. Pulling the club is the only way you can consistently ensure that you achieve the angles of the swing that you want. You want the club to be accelerating at impact, and the way to do this is to have your hands leading the shot with the centrifugal force still acting on the clubshaft. To do this, you have to aim the club, align your body to it, attach the left-hand grip, then the right-hand grip and establish the position of the ball at the stance while you are placing your feet in a square or open position. Then you can concentrate on your posture, making sure that your weight is established just behind the balls of the feet, your knees and hips are bent, and the calf and thigh muscles are supporting the weight of your body. By adopting this position you are creating a line in the plane of the swing.

Then, after a slight forward press, you recoil from it; turn your shoulders level to the ground and wind your left side until the hips are pulled around to accommodate the continuation of the shoulder turn around to 90 degrees so that at the top of the backswing, when you look at the ball, you are looking at it over your left shoulder. There is no point at the top of the backswing at which you are still, only a feeling of coiled power. The downswing is started by shifting the weight, turning the left hip to the left. This tightens the coil in the left side of the body and creates a whiplash effect in the downswing.

Centrifugal force releases the club through the ball, and you accommodate this by allowing your arms to rotate. At this stage of the swing keep your head positioned behind the ball. At the end of the follow-through, the left side of your body should be straight, the hips and shoulders level and your weight totally on the left side. The right foot

The equipment of a modern tournament professional: they need such large bags because they have to be prepared for every contingency, especially variable weather conditions.

should be resting lightly on the toes with the foot vertical. This simple technique, once it is practised and built into a confident skill, will be the soundest most reliable golf technique that you can adopt.

A GOOD SHORT GAME

The short game gives the most accurate measure of the quality of any golfer. Not even the greatest golfers hit all the greens, and the man who saves the most shots around the green will win. In an 18-hole round of golf, par allows for 36 putts. The best players rarely take more than 30. Putting does not require great strength, so it is within the physical capability of everyone to putt well. Concentration and application are all that are required to become proficient at half the game.

The routine for putting was described in Chapter 5, but it is worth summarizing here. First, change the grip, placing your thumbs down the top of the flat side of the grip. At address make sure you bend over far enough for your eyes to be directly above the ball to give you a proper perspective of the line the ball is required to roll along. Do not use your wrists during the putting stroke, and keep the putter head low to the ground. Follow through as far as you swing the club back in the backswing. Remember, however, that if your putting technique is successful and does not follow along these lines, stick with it. The holed putt does not know what technique was used.

Chipping is just a putting stroke played with a lofted club. All the elements of the technique are similar – head over the ball, club low to the ground, follow through as far as you swing the club back – and you can use the putting grip if you like. By chipping in this way you can relate to the "feel" or your unconscious ability to hit the ball at the desired speed that you have developed with your putting stroke. As the shot gets longer and the trajectory higher, you start to pitch with a longer swing, introducing just a little wrist action to the stroke. This helps to fly the ball up in the air, but the amount of work done by the body is still minimal.

In the discussion of sand technique, we discussed the importance of opening the clubface, swinging to the left of the target and letting the open clubface slice under the ball so that it flies out high. Practice to see how much you can open the clubface to see how high the ball will fly. Also practice wriggling your feet in the sand to learn to judge the texture, so that you know how hard to hit behind the ball.

All these techniques are part of the short game, and once you have mastered them you will soon notice the results on your scorecard.

SELF-APPRAISAL

If you want to be competitive, you have to be honest with yourself. It is no good pretending that you can boom the ball off the tee if you cannot. Sooner or later there will come a time when you will have to hit the ball that far. An honest man will accept his limitations and look for a way around the trouble. The man whose ego will not let him lay up, has to go for the shot, knowing in his heart of hearts that it is doomed to fail. It is important to go to the practice ground and measure the distances you can hit with all your clubs. Then you can fit your shots into the demands of the course. There should be a regular increment, probably between 8 and 12 yards, in the distance you can hit each club. The next problem is to find out which clubs you can hit straight and which you cannot.

If it is your game to slice 9 shots out of 10, it is pointless to aim straight down the middle of every fairway and hope that you hit the tenth shot straight. You must aim off to the left to allow for the sliced shot. This becomes vital in competition: if you aim straight and slice, you are going to finish up in the rough all the time and give yourself no chance of developing a score even though you might have a strong iron game or be good at putting. On a very narrow hole you might, with practice and analysis, decide that you can hit your 3 wood or your 5 wood straighter much more often than you can your driver because of the extra backspin that these clubs produce in the ball. In that case, on a very narrow hole, it makes sense to hit these clubs from the tee rather than go with your driver, which may very well get you 10 or 15 yards farther up the fairway but which, 50 per cent of the time, may have you farther in the rough.

So that you can analyze your own game, it is important that you record your scores whenever you play and in all circumstances. After your game, break down your scores into the number of greens you have hit in regulation, the number of putts you have taken on each hole, the number of times you got up and down out of a sand bunker in two, and the number of fairways you hit from the tee. This kind of analysis will soon show you where the weaknesses lie in your game. If you are hitting 12 to 14 greens in regulation but are still failing to break 80, your putting has to be looked at very closely. If you find that you are regularly shooting 30 putts a round but still only scoring in the 80s, you must look at your long game. When you analyze your long game, see how many drives hit in the fairway allow you shots to the green. If your shots to the green are good, but you are driving into the rough, the driver needs to be practiced.

It would also be interesting to know whether you found you had a greater success hitting the greens with a 5 wood than you did a 2 iron. If your long iron play is not very good and you hit a lot of greens with your 5 wood, it might be worthwhile introducing a 6 or 7 wood into your bag at the expense of the 2 or 3 irons. If you miss a lot of greens when you play, it might be worth dropping one of your long irons and introducing a third wedge to your set. A 60 degree wedge would be particularly useful if you like to use the solid, two-piece ball. It may be that the flight on your long irons is too low, and therefore, when you try to hit a shot of up to 220 yards into the green and have to carry it over water or sand, you would be better off playing that shot with a more lofted wooden club.

An honest analysis of your game will help you understand how to play your good shots and how to work to the strengths of your game.

ROYAL LYTHAM AND ST. ANNES GOLF CLUB

Date . 17 JULY 1988

Please replace divots, smooth bunkers and repair pitch marks.

M'krs Score	Hole	Yards	Par	Stroke Index	Gross Score A	Gross Score B	Points Win + Loss − Half O	M'krs Score	Hole	Yards	Par	Stroke Index	Gross Score A	Gross Score B	Points Win + Loss − Half O
	1	206	3	13	3				10	334	4	10	3		
	2	420	4	5	4				11	485	5	4	6		
	3	458	4	1	5				12	189	3	14	3		
	4	393	4	9	4				13	339	4	18	3		
	5	188	3	15	3				14	445	4	6	4		
	6	486	5	7	4				15	468	4	2	4		
	7	551	5	3	5				16	356	4	16	4		
	8	394	4	11	4				17	413	4	8	4		
	9	162	3	17	3				18	386	4	12	3		
	Out	3258	35		35				In	3415	36		34		
									Out	3258	35		35		
									Total	6673	71		69		

NAME(S)

A PAUL EALES   H'cap SCR   Strokes

B

HANDICAP   SCR   Won

NET SCORE   69   Lost

Result

Marker's Signature ....

Player's Signature ....

S.S.S. 73   Par 71

G2580

The postscript to a perfect round of golf is a properly marked scorecard. Learning to complete a scorecard correctly is just as important as learning to drive and putt well. The score on each hole must be clearly marked and any alterations initialled. Both the player and the marker must sign the card attesting that the score on each hole is correct.

STRATEGY

The first rule of strategy is that you must have a knowledge of the basic Rules of Golf. It would be surprising if anyone has a perfect knowledge of all The Rules and of all the decisions on those and of all the situations that can crop up in a round of golf. So the first and most important thing to put in your bag after your golf clubs is a copy of the rules. Any disputes or any doubts about the correct procedure can be sorted out on the spot. When aspiring professionals take the course that decides whether they can become a professional or not, they are not asked questions on the Rules of Golf as such, but are, instead, taught to use the book of rules. They are shown how to use the book and how to find the rule that they need to know rather than being asked direct questions on individual rules. No one wants to be a golf course lawyer, and a book of rules in your bag will save you from acquiring that sort of reputation.

The second point about strategy, or "course management" as Ben Hogan called it, is that it is very important to keep your ball in play. It doesn't matter if you take three or four shots to get to a green – at least by having your ball in play and on the green you can inflict some sort of pressure on your opponent – but if your ball is over the wall, out of bounds, or in the lake, then there is no pressure on him and the hole is his. On courses where there is an out of bounds or a lake or bad rough down one side of the hole, you should always tee up on the same side as the trouble. That way your shot will be angled away from it, and you will have a better chance of missing it. But when you aim away from trouble, don't aim at the hazards on the opposite side of the fairway. Ben Hogan is reported to have said that you should always aim at the grass, and what he meant was that if you are aiming at a fairway and you want to avoid trouble on one side, aim at the other side of the fairway, not off it. The same applies in the wind: aim on the edge of the fairway that the wind blows from; don't aim outside it. That way you can only ever get in trouble on the side that you are trying to avoid. When you aim at the green, aim at the left side or the right side, not at the bunkers. Then, unless you get a terrible mishit, you are always going to finish on the grass, as Hogan would say.

153

Matchplay strategy

In matchplay it is a good ploy to hit your tee shot short of your opponent's tee shot, so long as you can reach the hole. This will give you the advantage of hitting your second shot first, and if you hit a good shot and put your ball close to the hole, the pressure on your opponent is considerable. It makes his shot much harder. This ploy helps in a negative way too: if your opponent sees you hit a bad shot he may very well get sloppy himself. And when you get on the greens and your balls are equidistant from the hole, always putt first if you have the chance. Don't wait to watch him putt, because getting your shot in first gives you a tremendous psychological advantage.

You may be playing with an opponent who likes to play quickly, while you may prefer to play at a slower pace. Do not be bullied into playing more quickly than you need to; it's important that you try to maintain your own tempo. So many matches have been lost and won by players hurrying to keep up with a faster opponent or slowing down to keep back with a slower opponent. If your speed of playing is different from your opponent's, be determined to get him to play at your speed rather than be encouraged to play at his.

It is easy to become discouraged when you have missed a couple of shots together or you have hit a shot out of bounds, but it is important to keep trying. If a bad shot has eliminated your chances of making a par, you must try like

mad to get a bogey. If you miss your second shot to a par 4, try very hard to make sure that you don't take more than 5. You will usually hit the green with your third shot and leave yourself a putt for a par, and it's quite astonishing how often these shots go in. We've all met players who miss one shot and then give up on the hole. They allow one slight error to eliminate all their chances of recovery.

STRATEGIES FOR DIFFERENT STANDARDS

Bunker

Bunker

Bunker

Fairway

Rough

Tee

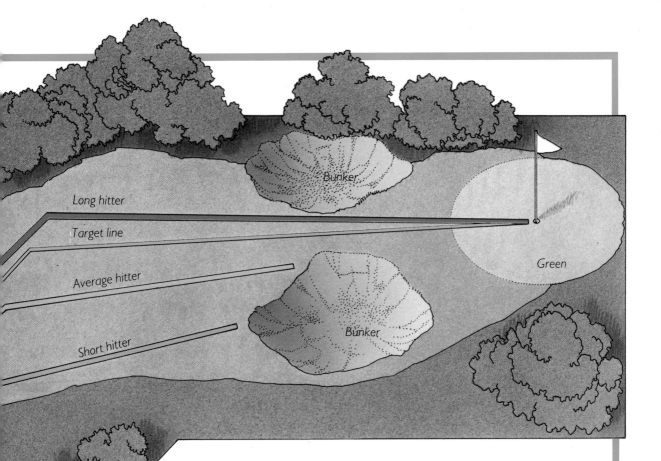

Long hitter

Target line

Average hitter

Bunker

Short hitter

Bunker

Green

THE LONG HITTER
On a long par four hole which doglegs to the right, the long hitter would tee the ball up on the left-hand side of the tee, angling the ball toward the corner of the dogleg, knowing that if the ball is hit slightly to the right the shot will still carry the corner. Leaving as short a shot as possible increases the chances of hitting the green in two shots.

THE AVERAGE HITTER
The average hitter will know on the tee that the green is out of range in two shots, so the main objective is to use the second shot to place the ball short of the bunkers guarding the green. The drive must be placed in the middle of the fairway and no great emphasis laid on length.

THE SHORT HITTER
The short hitter's chief requirement is to keep the ball on the fairway. Because his swing is relatively weak, rough presents a greater hazard than it does for the stronger player, and rough must be avoided at all costs.

155

8 EQUIPMENT

The history of the development of equipment is a fascinating subject and demonstrates man's ingenuity in creating more efficient clubs for hitting golf balls. The ball itself in its modern form is the result of sophisticated technology, and throughout the history of the game, alterations to the ball have caused many of the major changes in golf clubs. The right equipment is essential if you are to realize your full potential as a golfer, and modern golf club manufacturing techniques enable clubs to be found that will suit most golfers' physiques so that they have the best possible chance of success.

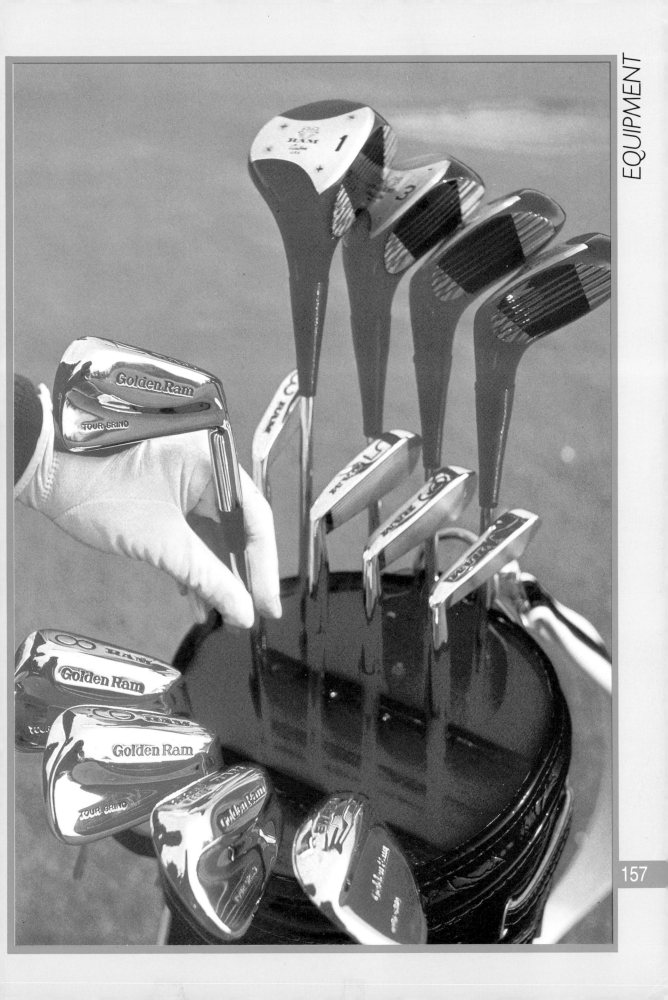

GOLF CLUBS

All golf clubs have three major components – head, shaft and grip – and the various specifications of these produce the feel of the club. It is important that a player understands how clubs work so that he can fit his clubs to his game rather than the other way round, and in so doing, play the game to the best of his ability rather than fighting the game with his clubs.

The early clubs were made with a long, thin wooden head, hickory shaft and thick leather grip. Over a period of time clubs with iron heads were developed, and these had more lofted faces than the woods and allowed the player to loft the ball more.

THE STEEL SHAFT

The first important development in club design occurred in the United States in the 1920s. This was the advent of the steel shaft, which greatly influenced the method of playing the game. Although the first steel shafts were available in the early 1920s, it was to be another ten years before they became widely used.

To understand the popularity of the steel shaft, it is necessary to understand the role of the shaft during the golf swing. Contrary to popular belief, the shaft bends and recovers only twice during the swing – first, at the top of the backswing when the club changes direction; secondly, at impact. The first bend is caused when the hands stop as they change direction, and the weight of the head keeps the momentum going longer, making the shaft bend. It straightens almost immediately the downswing begins. The second bend, which occurs at impact, is the vital one. Recent technology has shown that the dominant force during the downswing is centrifugal. This means that during the downswing, the weight of the clubhead pulls outward, away from the center of the player's swing. This is the force that uncocks the wrists and returns the player's arc to the original width he set up at address. This force travels along the line of the shaft, never across it; so the shaft does not bend until the clubhead makes contact with the mass of the stationary golf ball at impact. The impact slows down the head of the club, but the hands should be past the ball so that the shaft has to bend. As the shaft is bent back at impact, it twists a little, causing the clubface to open slightly, producing a gear effect on the ball. The softer the flex of the shaft – that is, the more easily it bends – the more hook spin is produced by the impact. For this reason it is important for stronger hitters to use stiffer shafts in their clubs, and for weaker hitters to use softer shafts.

The center of gravity of the head is not in line with the shaft, because the shaft is attached to the near end of the clubhead. Therefore, as centrifugal force dominates the downswing, the club's center of gravity tries to pull itself into the line of the hands, causing the shaft to bend very slightly downward, which makes the lie of the club a bit flatter than it was at address. This bend and twist, which is known as torque, is very subtle and controllable in steel shafts, but it is much more exaggerated in hickory. The

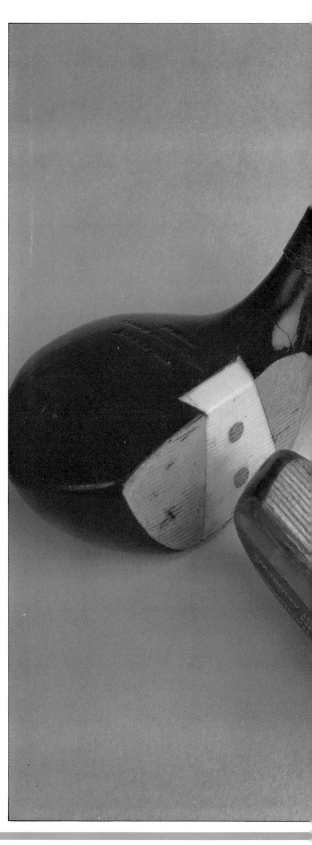

A selection of old clubs showing the different styles of the early club makers. Until the early 1930s, most clubs in Britain were made with hickory shafts; steel shafts were legalized in America in 1924. Many of these old clubs have become tremendously valuable among collectors.

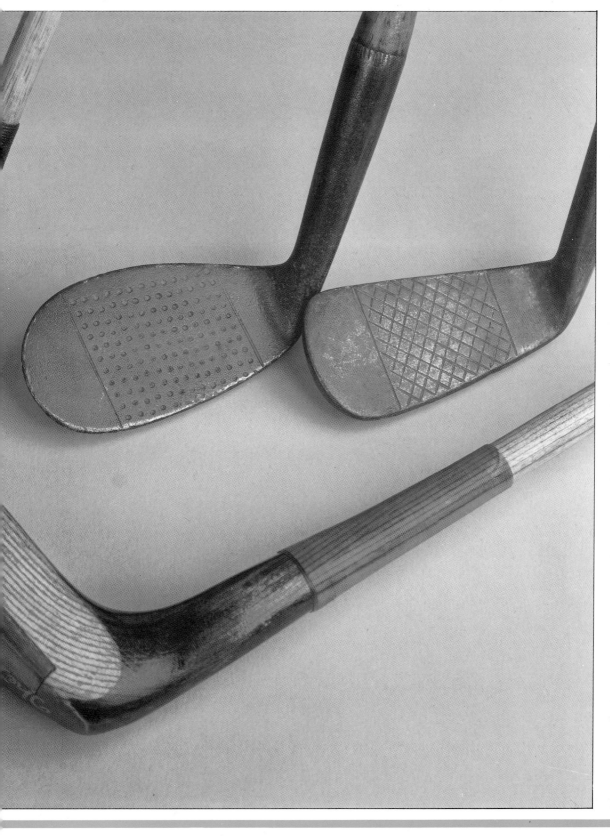

introduction of the steel shaft significantly improved the player's power and control during the swing.

Since the invention of steel shafts, various materials have been used and discarded by the manufacturers. Aluminum came, and went because it reduced the feel. Carbon fiber was expensive and had excessive twist, or torque, although it has now been improved vastly and is enjoying something of a revival. Titanium is too expensive for the benefit obtained from it. So, the ordinary steel shaft is the one that best suits the majority of players, provided they have the correct flex for their particular game.

TYPES OF FLEX

Each player has to decide which flex of shaft suits him or her best. Shafts are generally made in four flexes for men and two for women. The flex of the shaft is signified by the letter on the decal, which is fitted on the shaft with the maker's name. The letters are: X, which stands for extra stiff; S, which stands for stiff; R, which stands for regular; and A, which stands for flexible. The shafts on women's clubs are signified with the letters L for ladies and W for women, the latter having more flex than the L shaft.

When the shaft bends, the curve is dictated by the step-downs on the shaft. The closer the steps in the shaft, the lower the flex point, and the lower the flex point the higher the ball is flighted. In recent years there has been much controversy about whether there is an advantage for the handicap golfer to have the flex point high or low in the shaft. Although no firm conclusions have been reached, most manufacturers have designed shafts with a low flex point.

A recent development in shaft design has been the lightweight steel shaft. This is a breakthrough because it is 20-25 per cent lighter than the standard steel shaft. The weight saved in the shaft can be transferred to the head and be of much greater use to the golfer as the overall weight of the club does not have to change.

GRIP THICKNESS AND SWING WEIGHT

There are two basic grips available to the modern player: leather, which is traditional but harder to maintain in good condition, and rubber, which is easy to maintain and more usable in wet weather. Most clubs are fitted with rubber grips because they are convenient to use.

The thickness of the grip is of prime importance to the feel of the club. The thicker the grip, the more it weighs and therefore the lighter the head feels. Thick grips tend to restrict wrist action and are useful for any players who tend to flick at the ball with their hands. Thinner grips encourage wrist action, and the more hand action is available to the player, the heavier the head will feel.

The measurement that is used to describe this alteration in feel is known as "swing weight." Swing weight is a scale used by club-makers to measure the weight of the club relative to the length of the shaft. If all clubs had heads that weighed the same but shafts of different lengths, the clubs with the longer shafts would be heavier. To make all clubs feel the same weight, heads have to be made relatively heavier as the shafts get shorter. For example, for the

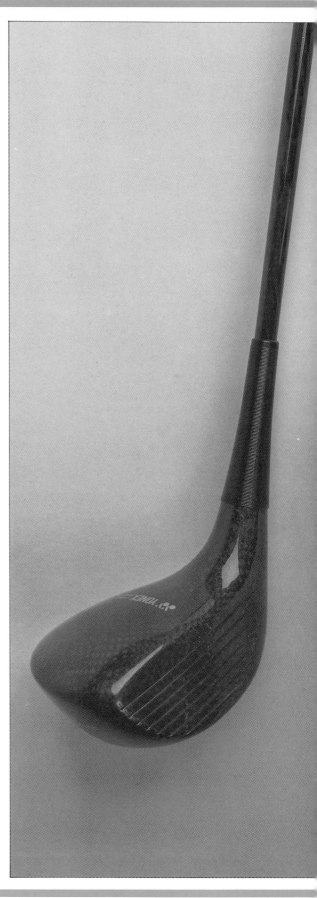

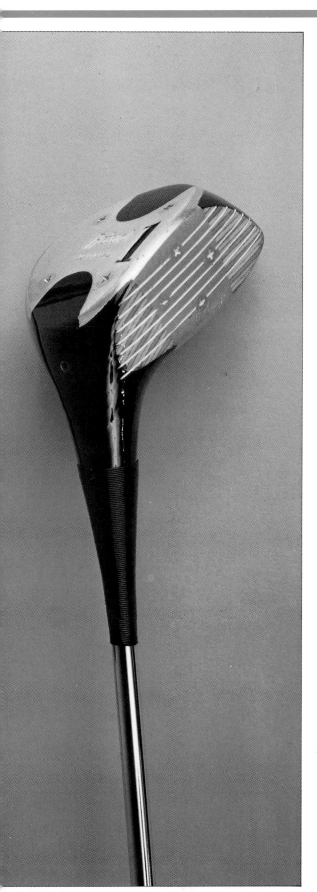

average man, the swing weight range is from C8, which is considered light, to D3, which would be heavy. Women's swing weight usually ranges from C4, which is light, to C9, which is heavy.

CHOICE OF HEADS

The heads of the wooden clubs have remained largely unchanged over the years. Those changes that have occurred have come with the different materials used as inserts, which have ranged from ivory to heavy plastics and to aluminum at various times. Woods are fitted with inserts because the continual striking of the same spot soon wears the head, and something more durable has had to be found to prolong the club's life. Until the 1950s, all heads were made of persimmon blocks, which, when dried out, produced a wonderful, hard, durable head. As demand increased, the quality of the available persimmon fell, and the heads cracked and warped. An alternative material was found in the shape of a laminated block of wood formed of several layers of plywood glued together. These blocks make hard, durable heads, with greater imperviousness to humidity and wear.

During the last five years we have seen a dramatic development in the design of wooden clubs with the increased popularity of "metal woods." These are woods with a hollow metal shell, which is sometimes filled with polystyrene. Many touring professionals use these clubs because they have a low center of gravity, which makes even the straightest of lofts easy to flight and which allows the professionals to hit drivers with 11 degrees of loft off the fairway. Metal woods have proved a godsend for the amateur player who has trouble hitting the ball in the air. An added bonus with metal woods is that all the weight of the club is around the outside, so that when the ball is struck there is less twist of the clubhead, which means the player can hit a straighter shot.

Iron heads are manufactured in two main ways. They are either forged or cast from steel. Forged irons are

Two examples of modern drivers. On the left is a driver of which both the shaft and head are made of carbon fiber. On the right is a more traditional steel shaft and wooden head with an aluminum insert.

The latest innovation in golf club design is the metal wood, which has a cast metal shell that disperses the weight into the perimeter of the clubhead, thereby enabling an off-center hit to be less damaging.

A set of metal woods, comprising numbers 1, 3 and 5. The shafts are made from steel and the heads are cast metal shells.
The driver (1 wood) is 43 inches long with 7 degrees of loft.
The 3 wood is 42 inches long with 13 degrees of loft.
The 5 wood is 41 inches long with 18 degrees of loft.

A set of traditionally styled woods of numbers 1, 3 and 5. The shafts are made from steel, and the heads are made from persimmon and fitted with a plastic insert.

The driver (1 wood) is 43 inches long and has 10 degrees of loft on the face.

The 3 wood is 42 inches long.

The 5 wood is 41 inches long with 21 degrees of loft.

Iron clubs are staggered in length and loft. They begin with the 3 iron, which has 23 degrees of loft, and increase in increments of 4 degrees up to the pitching wedge. The sand wedge usually has 55 degrees of loft.

The 3 iron is 38½ inches long and each club thereafter is successively half one-inch shorter.

3 iron   4 iron   5 iron   6 iron

7 iron · · · 8 iron · · · 9 iron · · · Pitching wedge

hammered out by craftsmen, who work the metal while it is hot, rather like a blacksmith with his anvil. This is the traditional way of making iron heads, and the quality of the club depends on the skill of the craftsmen.

Cast iron heads are manufactured by the lost wax method. This means that a set of heads is made up in a wax and from these a cast is made. Then the wax is melted – that is, "lost" – and poured off, and the manufacturer is left with an empty cast. This is then filled with molten steel and the iron head is cast perfectly. The advantage of cast iron heads is that the specifications can be more carefully monitored and measured and more consistent clubheads can be made.

Modern heads are attached to shafts merely with strong adhesive, but older clubs have a rivet through the shaft and hosel.

Much attention has been paid to heel and toe weighted irons. The underlying principle is that if a piece of steel were suspended in space and a ball bounced on it, the ball would bounce higher when it contacted the center of the bar. However, if weights were added to the ends of the bar, the bounce along the bar would be more consistent. By making clubs with extra weight at the ends – that is, heel and toe – the bounce off the area between these ends, the face, will be more consistent. The middle of the face is known as the sweet spot, and adding weight to the club's extremities enlarges this area, allowing better shots to be produced by off-center hits.

Average golfers find that clubheads with the weight placed near the sole are best. This type of blade has a low center of gravity, greater than the center of gravity of the ball, and this almost guarantees the ball will be flighted up

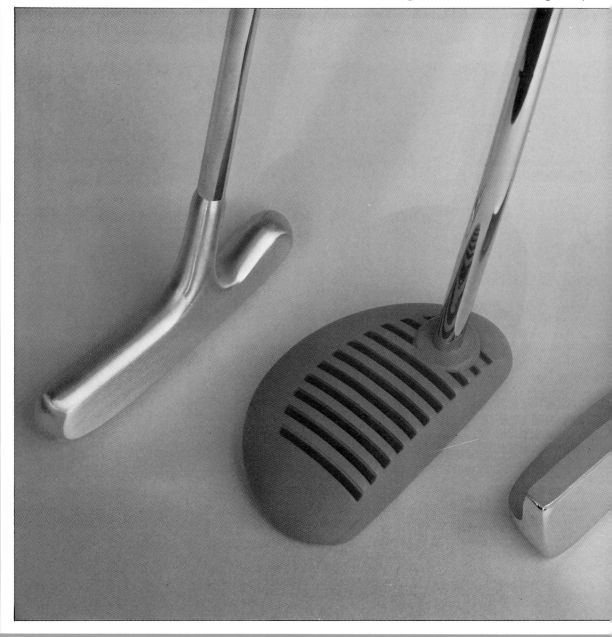

into the air. To this end the so-called "low-profile" club was introduced fairly recently. This is a very shallow-faced club, which was tremendously successful in the United States where the courses have a heavy, thick-bladed watered grass in which the ball tends to settle. Although the center of gravity helped to lift the ball out of this lush grass, in Britain these qualities tended to work against golfers playing from tighter lies in more windy weather, and their success has been somewhat limited in the UK.

CUSTOM-BUILT CLUBS

Go to any good professional shop and the range of clubs will amaze you. There are the sets lined up in regimented rows, head in, hosel out and grip in line with the seam of the next one, all gleaming like the Crown Jewels. Just the sight of all those shining shafts and highly polished woods sends a

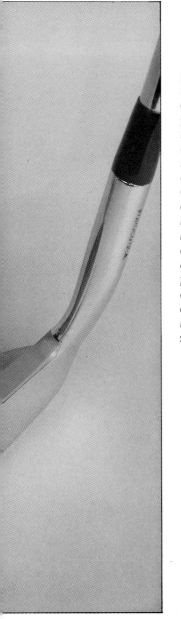

Three basic designs of putter: the brass-headed, center-shafted putter, the aluminum-headed mallet putter and the steel-headed blade putter. The center-shafted putter was invented at the turn of the century but banned in Great Britain until the early 1950s. The sight-lines on the top of the mallet putter are an excellent aid to aiming the club. The blade putter follows the same design as a conventional iron club, and many golfers find it lends itself to long, sweeping strokes.

shiver through most golfers' bank balances. However, it would be a mistake to think that just because a set of clubs is pleasing to the eye, it will be right for you. The clubs may look the best you have ever seen and you can picture yourself taking a course apart with them, as you have never done with your present ones, but wait a moment. The assistant at the counter may say that they are just the thing for you, but he is thinking about making a sale. It is far better to take the advice of your professional in his shop, or of the company's representative at an exhibition stand, about what will be the right makeup of clubs for your particular build and desires. After all, unless you always get all your clothes off the same rack, you wouldn't dream of getting married in anything but a made-to-order garment. The same applies to golf. If you want to improve and are anxious to become a top-class player, you are more likely to do so with a set of custom-built clubs, in other words, a set designed to fit you.

Like the tailor with his suits, making a set of golf clubs to fit the player is a specialized job. You have to go to the right place for the best results. The men who build such clubs are invariably craftsmen, who can turn the ugly chunk of persimmon or, as is more likely these days, the block of laminated wood, into the shapely head of a driver or 3 wood that will have most golfers drooling. But what do we mean by custom-built? The expression covers a multitude of things from the length and the grade of shaft to the right degree of loft and lie. You may think you know what is best for you, but after the experts have measured you and seen how you hit the ball, they could come up with some vastly different results. Grips, swing weight and inserts all come under the expert's eye, and you are bound to be surprised by what he comes up with for you.

Of course, if you are a beginner, custom-built clubs won't offer you any magic solution, but, on the other hand, starting out with made-to-order equipment could make the learning process a little less painful. If you are any sort of golfer, they are bound to make a difference. Just put yourself in the experts' hands and you can be sure it will do you good.

GOLF BALLS

The ball we play with has changed considerably over the years. Originally, golfers played with a leather-covered ball filled with boiled feathers, enough, it was said, to fill a top hat. This was superseded by a ball made from gutta percha, a substance obtained from latex. In 1902 Robert Haskell introduced the rubber-cored ball, which was eventually covered in balata. This was considered standard until the early 1970s, when surlyn, a more durable, synthetic cover was introduced. The introduction of surlyn coincided with the appearance of the two-piece ball, a surlyn-covered ball with a solid center. This ball, which is of equal density throughout, spins less than the rubber-wound ball, with its heavier center. The two-piece ball is now the top seller, as average golfers benefit more from the extra length the ball provides than they suffer from lack of control around the greens. In future it seems probable that a two-piece ball that will accept more spin will be developed, and the trend has already begun with the emergence of the lithium-covered ball.

Nowadays golf balls are no longer always white. They are now available in yellow and orange. Yellow balls benefit people with poor vision because they are more visible from a distance. They also appear to sit up out of the grass, and make the lie look better than it is, which boosts the player's confidence. Orange is easy to see in bright light but not quite so visible in gloomy conditions. The color is now dyed all the way through the cover, making scuffs and chips less visible and considerably increasing the life of the golf ball.

Compression is the measure of a golf ball's resistance to its deformation when it is hit. There is a scale of compressions, but this is a technicality that should not concern club golfers too much. If you want to test which compression of ball is best suited to your game, consult your club professional; otherwise don't get caught up with a complicated issue that is best left to the manufacturers.

The dimples on the golf balls are another topic of great discussion. The dimples are there to assist the ball's flight; their size and grouping determine certain qualities of the ball. Large dimples make the ball fly higher but mean that it has less run when it hits the ground. Small dimples bring a lower flight but more run. It's all a question of aerodynamics, which shouldn't worry the golfer too much, despite the marketing gimmick of the manufacturers.

CHOOSING A BALL

Which is the right ball for you? The answer might well be, the one that goes from tee to cup in par every time. Unfortunately, such a ball hasn't been developed yet. The ball that a professional uses may be totally unsuitable for your game. Apart from requiring ears to hear its master's commands to go left or go right, the golf balls used by professionals are normally suited to their individual game. They can derive the fullest benefit from a particular design of ball because their swing is consistent. The medium-to-high handicap player should choose a ball that suits his game or his particular course. He should not expect the ball to transform his game.

Feel has been mentioned on more than one occasion. Professionals like to use a balata-covered wound golf ball, but a surlyn-covered wound ball would be quite adequate for the average player who does not possess the professionals' skills. Such balls will also last a good deal longer since they are cut-resistant. New balls are expensive; so the average player may decide that it is unwise to splurge on a ball that, although designed to last for three or four rounds, may well be lost after three or four holes. He is more likely to play with any decent ball he has found – and why not?

The competent amateurs indulge in frequent needle matches with close friends, who nearly always want to gain maximum distance from the tee and control around the greens. The ideal ball for these circumstances would probably be a reputable wound ball – the compression and make of which being a matter of choice – or a two-piece ball. They may find a ball that goes a long way off the tee but dislike it because it feels hard when struck, and they might settle for a more pleasant feeling, if shorter flying ball. As we all know, it is hard enough to control a golf ball when it is perfectly round, so don't make it any more difficult by using one with a cut cover.

Finally, it is worth remembering that a ball is like a computer. Remarkable things can be done with it, but it must be told how to do it. Don't expect a ball to fly 180 yards and land next to the pin when its instructions are to swerve to the right and land in a bunker. Unfortunately this is true for all makes of ball. They are only as good as the person playing them.

The evolution of the golf ball from the featherie to the gutta percha to the Haskell rubber-cored ball to the modern solid-center ball. Dimple patterns have been developed over the years to produce maximum aerodynamic efficiency.

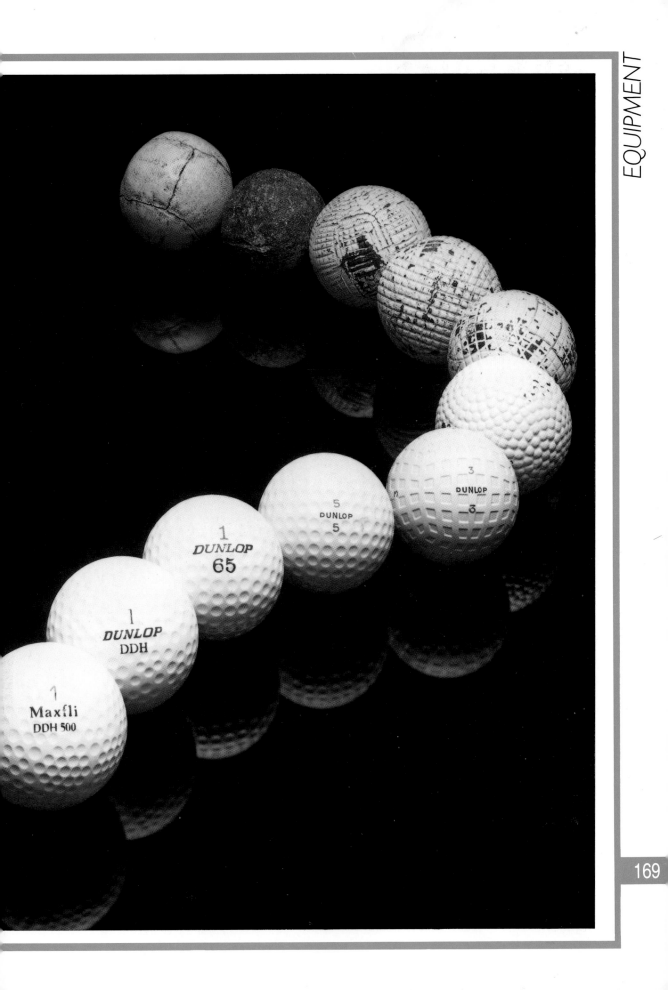

STARTER KITS

I t is not necessary for junior golfers to start the game with a full set of golf clubs. Three irons, a wood and a putter are quite sufficient for learning the basics of the game. Perhaps the best shot-maker of all, Severiano Ballesteros, learned to play using just one club, a 3 iron.

Playing with a limited number of clubs teaches youngsters to manufacture different shots with each club.

Adults starting the game can learn to play quite easily with half a set of second-hand clubs. This involves no great financial outlay and, should the player not take to the game, the outlay may be recovered.

A junior half-set comprising 5, 7 and 9 irons, a 3 wood and putter. These clubs are much shorter and lighter than adult clubs and suit a child's strength and stature.

CLOTHING

The first requirement of golf clothing is that it is comfortable. In recent years manufacturers have been so successful in designing stylish, colorful, comfortable clothing that many non-golfers have taken to wearing golf clothing as leisure wear. The modern fashion for intarsia-knit sweaters developed from golf leisure wear. The modern trend is toward sweaters and shirts that carry club crests or logos.

A selection of modern golf clothing. Sweaters, shirts and slacks can be coordinated in colors and styles, and shoes and golf gloves can also be matched. A golfer will walk further in golf shoes than in any pair of street shoes, so it is important that they should be soft and well-fitting but provide maximum support. A smartly turned out golfer has a psychological advantage before starting to play.

9 EVOLUTION OF THE GOLF SWING

This chapter defines the elements of the modern swing and describes how the swing has changed over the years, usually in response to developments to the club and ball. The changes in the swing are also analyzed, from the traditional, classic swing of yesteryear to the compact method used by today's top professionals.

◄ TARGET ►

To inform on the development of modern technique and how, through different eras, it has been the equipment which has determined technique. To provide an analysis of how the great players have refined technique in line with equipment development.

ACHIEVEMENT

An understanding of how the golf swing has evolved and a realization that it is still developing and can always be improved.

Craig Stadler, a former Masters Champion, playing from the 4th tee at Augusta.

FROM PUSH TO PULL

A study of the history of the golf swing reveals a dramatic difference between the methods used 100 years ago and those employed by the top stars of today. There are many reasons for this difference. Golfers are now stronger, healthier, better educated and, most important of all, better equipped. And it is the improvement in golf equipment, coupled with better technique and the introduction of the steel shafts, that have produced the major differences.

Before the use of steel, most shafts were made from hickory. Although it was the best material available at the time, hickory shafts caused a considerable amount of torque, between the grip and the head. To compensate for this torque, the early golfers developed a rolling, open, flat type of swing, which was the only way to accommodate the twisting of the clubface away from the grip. This type of action was initiated by opening the clubface at the very start of the backswing, and this was achieved by turning the whole of the body at once. Great importance was placed on an early hip turn, and the concept of turning in a barrel was born. This rotation of the whole body had the effect of swinging the club in a low arc immediately around the legs and very low to the ground. The ball was struck by rotating the hands rapidly through impact in concert with the twisting of the clubface, which had been opened so much in the backswing that the only way to get it squared up to the target at impact was to keep the body very still. This gave the arms and hands time to return the face of the club back to square in relation to the body.

When steel shafts were introduced, players found that they could extend the line of the swing much straighter back from the ball for a greater distance and also, after striking the ball, that they could keep the clubhead traveling toward the target further. This, of course, helped to keep the ball on line and produced more accurate shots. To find this wider, straighter arc, the clubhead arms would swing back, allowing only the shoulders to turn during the first half of the swing. This prevented the clubhead from turning inside around the legs too soon in the backswing and kept the club traveling in the plane of the swing, which was directed towards the target. The hips were permitted to rotate only enough to allow a full shoulder turn. This made it easier to leave the downswing with the hips and legs, allowing the powerful muscles in the back and legs to be brought into the swing.

When the lower half of the body is the source of power for the pull back through the ball, the club will try to find the place around the hips. This creates a slight looping of the club on its return path, allowing it to approach the ball from further inside the target line, a feature of the swings of such great golfers as Ben Hogan, Arnold Palmer, Lee Trevino and the late Tony Lema. This method is based on the concept of coiling the left side in the backswing and uncoiling it in the downswing. With the left side in control, the club has to be pulled through the ball.

Bobby Jones at the peak of his competitive career. His swing was built on the performance of the hickory shaft, which twisted as the club was swung. To accommodate the torque in the shaft, the players had to use a flat, rolling-type swing which contained a lot of hip turn on the backswing. This movement kept the club low and then lifted it into a better plane by cocking the right wrist sharply as the club arrived at the top. In the picture, Jones is at the end of the swing and it is possible to see how the follow-through is the mirror image of the movement described above. The hips and shoulders have both turned the same amount and the cock of the wrists is obvious. The classic position of the straight left side and right foot are still desirable in modern technique.

THE PUSHER'S SWING

The pusher type of swing still retains several elements from the early days, especially when it comes to hip turn. The average pusher's grip shows two knuckles on the left hand, and the stance is fairly narrow to help promote a full hip turn. The backswing is initiated by moving the right hip and shoulder backwards or behind the player. The hips turn as far as possible, pulling the left heel high off the ground, before the physical act of keeping the left toe on the ground stops them turning any further. When the hips stop turning, the shoulders continue, and they turn until they can turn no further. The right leg normally straightens in the backswing, with the arms swinging up from the flat takeaway and the left wrist cupping at the top, opening the club face from the plane of the swing. At the completion of the backswing, the body has effectively just spun to the right. The downswing begins when the left heel is planted back on the ground and the bodyweight transferred back to the left side. The ball is struck by bracing the left side, with the arms and hands swinging the club past the body, which is held square to the target line. Using the pusher's method, the arms and hands are forced to rotate rapidly as the club passes the body so that they can square up the club face to the target at impact. The follow-through is narrow, with hands and arms winding close to the shoulders.

THE PULLER'S SWING

The other method, which I prefer and which I will call the puller's action, results when the left hand grip is a little stronger — showing two-and-a-half or three knuckles to the observer standing directly in front of the player — and the stance is a little wider than the shoulders to help restrict the hip turn. The club is pushed away from the ball with the left hand and shoulder, leaving the hips in their address position. When the shoulders have turned 45 degrees, they tighten the muscles down the left side of the body to the point where the taut muscles pull the hips into action. At the top of the backswing the shoulders will have turned 90 degrees, but the hips should not have turned more than 45 degrees. With the shoulder turn the weight is transferred to the inside of the right leg, and the backswing sequence begins with the arms, followed by the shoulders turning, then the hips turning, pulling the leg across and finally, if you are not supple enough to keep it on the ground, the left heel being pulled half an inch into the air. The downswing is initiated by the left hip clearing the ground to the left, pulling the shoulders and arms and followed by the club. This action produces a feeling of flying a backhand strike through the ball. At the finish of the swing, the left side is straight with the hips and shoulders level, the club is in the same relative position to the left shoulder in the follow-through as it was to the right shoulder at the top of the backswing, confirming that the through play is the same as the backswing. The back of the left hand and arm remain in line throughout the swing.

Left *Ben Hogan at the top of the backswing is balanced perfectly and in a perfect position to pull the club through the ball and toward the target. Because his hips have turned less than his shoulders, they are able to lead the pull of the left side during the through swing.*

Above *Judy Rankin's end of swing position is a perfect lesson to all golfers. Although small and petite, she has relied on swing discipline and balance to provide the distance she needs on this full-wood shot. A beautiful poised finish.*

179

Right *Jack Nicklaus, probably the greatest competitor golf has known, at the top of the backswing. Nicklaus is predominantly a body player; he twists his shoulders and hips further around than most professionals. The bigger hip turn makes him use his very strong legs more in the swing. This is his power source.*

Above *Nicklaus' power when striking the ball carries the club so far into the follow-through that the shaft hits his shoulder. His balance is perfect.*

Four giants of the modern swing: Bernhard Langer **(left)**, Seve Ballesteros **(below right)**, Ian Woosnam **(below)** and Greg Norman **(right)**. All four players are products of modern teaching methods. The similarity between their swings is no accident. Although the players are of different builds they all observe the correct fundamentals: they control the swing with their left side; they use their shoulders more than their hips, and their follow-through is wider than their downswing.

EVOLUTION OF THE GOLF SWING

Top left *Curtis Strange has pulled the club through the ball, and his hands are in the process of crossing over at hip height in the follow-through.*

Left *Tom Watson approaching impact. The angle of the camera reveals how much of his left hip is leading the unwind of the body.*

Above At the top of the backswing, Nick Faldo's left side is in full control. His shoulders have turned more than his hips which will lead in the backswing, pulling the club through the ball toward the target.

Faldo spent two years in the mid-80s rebuilding his swing under the direction of teacher David Leadbetter, to make it more reliable. He previously kept the clubface shut and lifted the club steeply in the backswing. This gave him a flail-type action when he changed direction, which led to inconsistencies. He worked on a more open, shallow takeaway which allowed him to gather his wrist cock throughout the whole of the backswing rather than for it to occur at the top. This calmer action proved worth the time and effort when Faldo won the Open at Muirfield in 1987.

GLOSSARY

Address
The position assumed by the player in preparing to make his or her swing.

Apron
Grass bordering the putting green that is cut shorter than the fairway but longer than the green.

Away
The ball furthest from the hole is away and is played first.

Backspin
A reverse spin which causes the ball to fly and stop quickly on the green.

Backswing
The initial movement of the club away from the ball until it reverses direction and moves into the downswing.

Birdie
One stroke less than the designated par for a hole.

Blade
A type of putter.

Block
The name given to the movement to prevent the clubface from turning naturally through impact.

Bogey
One stroke more than the designated par for the hole.

Break
The amount a ball will deviate from a straight line when putting across a slope.

Bunker
A depression in the ground usually filled with sand.

Caddie
A person hired to carry a player's clubs.

Carry
The distance from where the ball is hit to where it first lands.

Chip shot
A short shot played from the edge of the green. It flies low and rolls most of its distance.

Closed face
When the blade of the club points to the left of the target.

Closed stance
When the player's feet point to the right of his target.

Clubhead
The part of the club used to hit the ball.

Cocking the wrists
The bending of the wrists during the backswing.

Cut shot
A high sliced shot that flies softly and does not roll far after landing.

Divot
A piece of turf sliced out of the ground by the player's stroke.

Dogleg
A section of the fairway that does not run in a straight line but bends.

Downswing
The penultimate movement in the swing sequence when the club makes contact with the ball.

Draw
A subtle right-to-left shot.

Drive
To hit the ball from the tee.

Driver
The number 1 wood, which features the least loft on the clubhead.

Fade
A controlled shot hit with a slightly left-to-right flight.

Fairway
The mowed area of the course between the tee and the green.

Flagstick
The removable pole with flag attached showing where the hole is cut.

Flange
The part of the sole of the clubhead that protrudes at the back.

Flat swing
A swing which carries the club in an arc low around the body.

Follow-through
The part of the swing arc after the ball is struck.

Green
The most closely mowed part of the course in which the hole is cut.

Grip
The cover wound over the top part of the shaft. The hold of the hands on club.

Handicap
The number of strokes a player receives in order to reduce his score to par.

Hole
The hole is 4¼ inches in diameter and cut in the green. The individual section on a course from tee to green.

Honor
The right to hit first from the tee.

Hook
A shot that bends drastically from right to left in flight.

Insert
A piece of material let into the face of wooden clubs.

Iron
A club with a metal head.

Lie
The position in which the ball rests after being hit. The angle between the shaft and the sole of the club.

Line
The intended direction of the shot.

Loft
The angle at which the clubface points into the air.

Open face
When the clubface points to the right of the target.

Open stance
When a player's feet point to the left of the target at address.

Out of bounds
Ground from which play is prohibited.

Par
The number of strokes allowed on a hole for a good player.

Pitch
A short high shot to the putting green.

Pitch-and-Run
A shot similar to the pitch but played with a less lofted club.

Plugged lie
When the ball pitches straight into the ground and buries itself.

Pull
A shot hit straight but to the left of the target.

Punch
A low shot.

Push
A shot hit straight but to the right of the target.

Putt
When the ball is rolled along the ground with a straight-faced club.

Rough
Grass which is not cut short.

Round
Playing the full course.

Run
The distance the ball travels after hitting the ground.

Sand wedge
A club designed to recover from sand bunkers.

Set
The 14 clubs.

Short game
The shots of putting, chipping and pitching.

Slice
A shot that bends from left to right.

Sole
The bottom of the clubhead.

Square stance
When at address a player's feet are parallel to the target line.

Stance
The position of the feet.

Swing
The movement used to hit the ball.

Takeaway
The beginning of the backswing.

Tee
The area from which the ball is driven. A wooden or plastic structure on which the ball is placed before driving.

Top
A stroke hitting the ball above its center.

Turn
The rotation of the body during the backswing.

Upright swing
A lifting of the club in a high arc over the player's head.

Wood
A club with a wooden head.

Yardage chart
A small booklet of maps of the holes showing measurements from bunker, trees and so on.

USEFUL ADDRESSES

Golf Club & Golf Ball Mfs. Assn.
1150 S. US Hwy. One
Jupiter, FL 33477
(305) 744-6006

Golf Manufacturers & Distributors
Assn.
P.O. Box 37324
Cincinnati, OH 45222
(513) 631-4400

Golf Superintendents Assn. of
America
1617 St. Andrews Drive
Lawrence, KS 66044
(913) 841-2240

Golf Writers Assn.
of America
P.O. Box 37324
Cincinnati, OH 45222
(513) 631-4400

International Golf Assn.
625 Madison Ave
New York, NY 10022
(212) 872-9104

Ladies Professional Golf Assn.
4675 Sweetwater Blvd.
Sugar Land, TX 77479
(713) 980-5742

National Collegiate Athletic Assn.
U.S. Hwy. 50 & Nall Ave.
Shawnee Mission, KS 66222
(913) 384-3220

National Golf Foundation
1150 S. US Hwy One
Jupiter, FL 33477
(305) 744-6006

PGA World Golf Hall of Fame
P.O. Box 1908
Pinehurst, NC 28374
(919) 295-6651

Professional Golfers Assn.
of America
P.O. Box 109601
Palm Beach Gardens, FL 33410
(305) 626-3600

PGA TOUR
Sawgrass
Ponte Vedra Beach, FL 32082
(904) 285-3700

Royal Canadian Golf Assn.
RR #2
Oakville Ont. L6J 4Z3 Canada
(416) 844-1800

United States Golf Assn.
Golf House
Far Hills, NJ 07931
(201) 234-2300

Western Golf Assn.
Golf, IL 60029
(312) 724-4600

INDEX

*Page numbers in italic
refer to the illustrations*

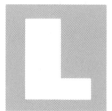

Unless otherwise indicated all photographs by Phil
Sheldon; with many thanks to him and his assistant Jan
Traylen. Pp76-77 Nottingham University; pp178-179
Golf Illustrated. All illustrations are by James Robins, with
the exception of pp34-39 which are by Nicholas
Hewetson.